Natural Intelligence

The Technology of Peace

Jim Gale

Cory Edmund Endrulat

Featuring Personal Testimonies by:
Kevin Fretz
Pat Miletich
Marjory Wildcraft
Joel Salatin
Rowdy Meyer
McKinley Hlady

A special thanks to those who are actively engaging in the solutions detailed in this book...

Lisa Mollison, Bill Bilodeau, Koreen Brennan, Sacred Lands Anderson Family, Marcel Jahnke, Mike Adams, Cameron James, Marcos Lopez, Carlos, Allen Campbell, Matthew Britt, Charles A. Thompson, Dr. Darrell Wolfe, Doc Wil Spencer, David Rodriguez, John Baxter, Broken But Beautiful Ministries, Inc., Mark Passio, Larken Rose, Brian Hickok, Brian Young, Andre Norman, Theo Fleury, Florida United, The Endrulat family, The Health Revealed Team, John Penuel Chidester III, Producer Mike (Aphix), The Gale family.

A special dedication to:

Isolda Clara Siclinda Wolfe Letenbauer Hagen Gale & Patrick James Gale

ISBN: 9798342924788
Copyright 2024 Cory Edmund Endrulat & Jim P. Gale

The Roots:

Please give time and consideration to this work.

The problem and solution to everything in our world is detailed here, in a way that is both step-by-step and concise.

To our families, to our future,
With you, in the present.

1

The Idea

"There is one thing stronger than all the armies in the world, and that is an idea whose time has come"
- Attributed to Victor Hugo

What is the idea? What does that mean?

The idea we have now, will change life forever for the future. We may say that the best idea is that which integrates all the best ideas, and this is what it means to stack functions. But what *really* is that idea? And what does it look like? Is it being utilized today? Has it ever been utilized before? If the idea is so good, why hasn't the idea gotten attention or become mainstream?

If the idea is relevant to the times we live in, let us reflect and ask ourselves...

What is it that the world truly needs?

What is it that the world loves or fears?

Perhaps we may observe the common struggles and concerns in the world...

War, Political Corruption, Scarcity, World Hunger, Food Insecurity, Mental Illness, Cancer, Heart Disease, Infertility, Environmental Pollution and Deforestation, Poverty and Unemployment, Mass Extinction, Tyranny, The Rise of Artificial Intelligence.

These may be the world's biggest problems.

However, we may describe the prison walls all day, and never come to actually consider escaping the prison. Where people do not know *how* and *why* to engage with new ideas, or have yet to hear of them, they may talk long about the problems of the world. Yet, *solutions do exist* among them. Many may see a hopeless doom, but others see an idea which can change the world overnight. They may be among the few who have the spark of light or spirit within them, they see the better tomorrow. They are the *visionaries* with the idea whose time has come.

We may blame greed or selfishness for the problems of our world, but what if we can turn these on it's head?...

What if we can be selfish or greedy in wanting to solve the world's biggest problems?

Instead of endless symptom management, with replacing a greater evil with a lesser evil, or excusing any evil we recognize, we must learn and be able to get to the root cause, to treat the whole condition of the evil. The evil no longer needs to be an evil, the problem can become the solution. *All it takes is one idea, one vision.*

Is it easy? Anything new we learn takes persistence and time. It if it's meant to be, it will be when the time is right. The demand will be apparent, the ideas will become irresistible. It will spontaneously grow, and the message will become easy over time. With simply the right idea at the right time, the needs will be dissolved and the problems solved. One idea to the next, one vision to the next, new realities are formed.

The masses of people follow the primary philosophies and ways of living, the old ideas. This conformity is challenged by new ideas, which comes as necessary to fulfill the balance in fixing the old and inefficient systems. We see the *greater* ideas by being able to challenge one idea with the other. Change is often accompanied by resistance, but this *too* can change. Fear and cognitive dissonance may occur in people, but so does critical thinking, inspiration and motivation. We cannot hide from what's to come. We must do what we both *know* and *feel* must be done. We all live in the same reality as philosophers and great spiritual teachers. They observed ever-present truths and shared them with the people, often at odds with the powers that be. They did not operate in fear, they gathered faith and energy around their cause, enough to make history indefinitely. *We are making history now, and you can be a part of it.*

People yearn for solutions, but simultaneously fear having to put them into effect. They tell themselves they don't know, or that it's too much work, or that others will judge or doubt them. This doesn't need to be. Every cloud has a silver lining, we have only to see it.

2

The Mind

"Whatever the mind can conceive and
believe, it can achieve."
- Napoleon Hill, Author of Think and Grow Rich

What can our mind conceive and believe?
Was he wrong?

Many may have thought that technology as
we have it now, would take much longer to be
developed, or that it may not even be developed
at all. Yet, humanity has done it as the great
momentum of the species has emphasized its
possibilities. Stronger than all the armies of the
world, was *the idea* for technology which would
eventually change the entire way an army would
operate overall, for instance. The idea of creating
a nuclear explosion which can destroy entire
cities and nations in one sweep, became a stark
reality as people put their time and energy into
envisioning and creating it.

Everything that has been created had to first be thought of in *the mind*. The hermetic *principle of mentalism* states that...

"the all is mind. The universe is mental. Thoughts lead to the manifestation of things and events. Thoughts create our state of existence and the quality of our experience. We may be responsible for everything we create by being responsible for everything we think."

Using your mind but opening your heart, reflect upon the use of your mind...

What do you think of on a daily basis?

Do you ever try to think about better ways of doing things within your own life?

Do you ever want to learn something new?

Do you ever imagine a better life?

Our reality is based on our actions, and our actions are based on our mindset. There have been many studies done on how our mentality can greatly affect our health, for example. Researchers like Bruce Lipton and Joe Dispenza bring this even further. Mental health as a whole has become a great concern for many people. We also know that many visionaries such as Mahatma Gandhi, Martin Luther King Jr. and Bob Marley have told us that "mental slavery" is the root cause to *all forms* of slavery, or the most important to address.[1] Even these mere terms and concepts that we use and create, are formed from the mind to help us form summaries, achieve greater works and new forms of practice, different ideologies, philosophies and so forth.

Republics, Democracies, Communism, Capitalism... The list goes on, we have conceived them to the point where they become almost one with our reality. For better or for worse overtime, we've managed to achieve anything we set our minds to. Most especially when many individuals have the same mentality together in mass.

Without the introduction of new ideas for our minds to conceive, we become stagnant. We cannot innovate without challenging the old or thinking outside the box. We can *never* truly improve as a human species so long as we aren't willing to see and imagine what is possible. Ask yourself...

Can I conceive and believe being happy, strong, vibrant and connected?

[1] Refer to "Slavery Gone For Good: Black Book Edition" by Cory Edmund Endrulat, featuring 200+ Philosophers, Former Slaves, Abolitionists, 100+ Quotes, Historic Excerpts

Can I be on the highest level of the Hawkins scale?[2]

We may define freedom as infinite possibility. Therefore, the fear of freedom is the death of imagination. When you have an inspired idea, an idea that makes you feel alive, great and motivated, a new idea that blows your mind, where do those ideas come from? They do not come from a stressed out mind. The acronym for "FEAR" is "False Evidence Appearing Real." Dismissing this as merely "corny" has the same effect, because people sometimes want to hold onto their fear and therefore deny possibility. They will argue for their fear and dismiss or fight those who show a different reality in their projection, but only they can truly free themselves from this fear. We attain freedom and see the possibility, when we value ourselves and provide ourselves with a sense of enlightenment.[3]

We do not need to stay in the dark of ignorance and deception, merely *order-following*

---

[2] The Hawkins Scale as detailed in the works of David R. Hawkins, M.D., Ph.D. Another relevant work includes "Power vs Force: The Hidden Determinants of Human Behavior."

[3] Finding meaning, inspiration, value or purpose within our lives can be a pyschotherapeutic method to overcome evil and reach our greatest ability. "Man's Search for Meaning" by Viktor Frankl helps to emphasize this relationship.

and relying *only* on the "experts" and the order-givers, leading our lives astray because they don't live our *own* lives. It is time not for *govern-mente[4]* or *mind control*, but *empower-mente, enlight-mente* or *self-government*, mental empowerment and sovereignty.[5] We can recognize this *natural intelligence*, which includes our conscience[6] in choosing right from wrong, promoting the solutions that will create life and discouraging the problems that suppress it and create evil. Life expands and nurtures, evil contracts and coerces. We have the ability to change our *own* reality. Only from *self-ownership*, or the knowledge of how to live happily and healthily without restraint and hindrance, can someone be free. As former slave and Abolitionist Frederick Douglas shares with us...

"To make a contented slave, you must make a thoughtless one. It is necessary to darken his moral and mental vision, and, as far as possible,

---

[4] The word "government" may be attributed to the Latin verb *gubernare or guverno,* meaning "to control" and the Latin noun *mens or mentis,* meaning "mind."

[5] The word "sovereign" may be attributed to the Latin adverb *super*, meaning "above" and the Latin noun *regnum,* meaning "rulership, control."

[6] The word "conscience" may be attributed to the Latin prefix *con*, meaning "together" and the Latin verb *sciere*, meaning "to know, to understand."

to annihilate his power of reason. He must be able to detect no inconsistencies in slavery. The man that takes his earnings, must be able to convince him that he has a perfect right to do so. It must not depend upon mere force; the slave must know no Higher Law than his master's will. The whole relationship must not only demonstrate, to his mind, its necessity, but its absolute rightfulness."

Therefore, freedom is *the idea* that keeps on giving. Most people *know* freedom is important, the question is do we know *how exactly* to attain and exercise freedom? In other words, how do we practice *self-ownership* and create that happy and healthy world and self?

Humanity has experienced many different times and centuries of different ideas, grappling with the world's biggest problems, and realizing the importance of freedom. There were times where certain groups of people were oppressed more than others. There were times where chattel slavery was considered a natural and essential part of life. There were times where society condemned those who appeared to be witches, or exhibiting certain traits and victimless behaviors. In America, it was considered a radical idea to want to get rid of the Monarchy after thousands of years. Similarly, it was considered a radical idea for the Abolitionists to want to get rid of chattel slavery.

With one simple "radical"[7] idea, the world can change radically. And at the end, that idea is no longer seen as radical.

Time tells the true victor.

---

[7] The word "radical" may be attributed to Latin *radicalis*, "of or having roots." Etymology from the 14th century suggests "originating in the root or ground" or "virtual to life." The figurative meaning as "going to the origin, essential."

3

The Solution

"Though the problems of the world are increasingly complex, the solutions remain embarrassingly simple."
- Bill Mollison, Founder of Permaculture

Why are the problems so complex?
What are the simple solutions?

Many of us may have experienced how the "problems" can pull us down a rabbit hole, but we also come to realize overtime just how simple the solution is. As the solutions are ignored, the problems increase and as the problems increase, the solutions may become further overshadowed though simultaneously increasingly evident. In other words, when we are stuck on the problems, we may continue managing the symptoms, making the problems increasingly complex as we still have not *actually* fixed the problem itself. As things get worse and worse, problems that don't need to be problems are created, and it is clear that the solutions have yet to be realized. The idea whose time has come could be conceived and therefore achieved, if we are able to simply lift the veil. Otherwise, we feel limited, hopeless and fearful. The so called "radical" ideas were really just fundamental ideas that for long went unrecognized or ignored, despite being seemingly obvious once they were innerstood and embraced. We can laugh at our silly past, but also often find ourselves asking "how could we have ever done that?"

Change-makers throughout history were often labeled and attacked as utopian[8] and impractical. Yet, those who saw their ideas, saw their necessity, educated others, and it was done. It became mainstream, and the past looked foolish, the present became the new reality. It took *faith, love and courage.* It certainly did for

---

[8] Emma Goldman said "Every daring attempt to make a great change in existing conditions, every lofty vision of new possibilities for the human race, has been labeled Utopian" Alan Watts said "I am trying to make the deadly serious point that, as of today, an economic utopia is not wishful thinking but, in some substantial degree, the necessary alternative to self-destruction." Oscar Wilde said "A map of the world that does not include Utopia is not worth even glancing at, for it leaves out the one country at which Humanity is always landing. And when Humanity lands there, it looks out, and, seeing a better country, sets sail. Progress is the realisation of Utopias."

the *his-story* of Jim Gale from Food Forest Abundance, think of this...

Born in Minnesota, from the beginning, as a child, Jim Gale was known as "nature boy" because he spent a lot of time in nature and playing with animals such as frogs and snakes. His favorite show was Omaha's "Wild Kingdom" and his only magazine subscription ever was "Ranger Rick." After high-school, Jim had a wrestling coach who wanted him to write his goals. At first reluctant, he listened to Dennis Waitley, author of *The Psychology of Winning*, which inspired and influenced him to set out to become a 3-time all American wrestler and national champion after individuals doubted him and thought it was impractical. As Jim conceived of winning, and embodied it, he made it his reality. He then moved to Hawaii for 4 years and got into bartending, but he wanted to see the world and do something more with his life. At 29, he started to backpack around the world in 37 countries, which included living with the Maasai tribe in Africa, visiting the Karachi in Pakistan and Chiang Rai in the Jungle. He set his new goals to make money, reading books about vision and inspiration. He read everything he could find regarding human performance, especially during his journey. Jim later met a friend who he worked with in a mortgage company, which 3 years later from scratch, generated about $1.3 billion in gross revenue, leading him to retire when he was 32 or 33 years old as he also got sick of the industry. He then bought a boat and lived on the ocean in the Bahamas for a year, but got bored quickly because there wasn't the feeling of *inspiration* he had imagined. He decided to move to Costa Rica and learned about the word "permaculture" which means "permanent culture." When he studied this, he realized it's a sustainable agricultural design science which the world does not know about. With this powerful revelation, he saw that we were destroying life on multiple levels, from our air, to our water, to our soil and so on. Jim spent over two years digging into this problem, a never ending rabbit-hole, and it did not feel good to him seeing how badly things have become. He realized how much he loved nature, his family and their future, and he developed optimism with faith, love and courage to focus on the solution rather than the problem, as he innerstood that it is embarrassingly simple in comparison. Jim pondered on creating a business model which can be scalable, serving the whole world based on the solution, forming Food Forest Abundance.[9]

---

[9] Food Forest Abundance as founded by Jim Gale. "Grow Your

Therefore, throughout all of Jim Gale's journey, in the end, he found the idea which inspired him, the embarrassingly simple solution whose time has come that is stronger than all the armies of the world, which we can conceive and achieve...

We need to take the poisons out and
grow food instead of lawns.
Mass adoption through Permaculture Food
Forests would catalyze a shift in awareness.

Then, we bring all the best ideas together with
this idea, through initiatives and outreach.
We reach out to the influencers around the world.
We engage and strengthen the structure of this
idea through what may be known as
the The Council of 12.

Permaculture[10] is a revolutionary and holistic design system aimed at creating sustainable and self-sufficient human environments by mimicking the patterns and relationships found in natural ecosystems.

Eden: Transform Your Space into a Thriving Food Forest" https://foodforestabundance.com/ A helpful interview may include Jim Gale with Del Bigtree on The Highwire

[10] Permaculture, as defined with principles, ethics and design techniques, can be explored in "Introduction to Permaculture" by Bill Mollison and Reny Mia Slay. Expanding on the concepts, may be found in "Gaia's Garden" by Toby Hemenway.

Coined by Bill Mollison and David Holmgren in the 1970s, the term combines "permanent agriculture" and "permanent culture," reflecting its focus on long-term ecological health and cultural resilience. Permaculture integrates traditional and modern principles from ecology, energy conservation, landscape design, and environmental science to create systems that are multifunctional, bio-diverse, ecologically sound, economically viable, and capable of meeting their own needs without destroying or polluting the environment.[11] By emphasizing thoughtful observation and working with nature rather than against it, permaculture seeks to maximize productivity and minimize waste, providing sustainable systems that benefit both humans and the planet. It is cooperation over competition, and long-term sustainability over short-term exploitation. Permaculture is therefore not just *the* solution, it is our very survival and optimal condition, it is the inevitable future.

---

[11] In 1971, the U.S. was taken off the gold standard by the government, ending the Bretton Woods system, leading to the "Nixon Shock." In 1973, there became significant economic turmoil, a stock market collapse occurs. In the 1970s, farmers dealt with rising costs, falling commodity prices and high interest rates. In response, chemical fertilizers, pesticides and other technologies were promoted and used.

4

The Change

"You never change things by fighting the existing reality. To change something, build a new model that makes the existing model obsolete"
- Buckminster Fuller

What is the new model for society? How can we abandon the old reality?

We don't need to be stuck any longer on the old systems which don't truly serve us, when we can conceive the new system which proves itself. We don't need to fight existing reality, if we work from where we are, accepting the challenge. Only from accepting things as they are, can we move on for the better, just as we may learn from history for the future betterment of humanity. If we know people's current concerns, we may consider for instance, what they will yield, literally, from the solution whose time has come. How about this for return on investment...

A seed or stick can produce millions and millions of meals over the next ten years. The one simple sweet potato vine with 2 leaves at the end, can produce 100 pounds in the next 18 months. You take 10 minutes to use your hands to dig a hole and put that vine in the ground. You add irrigation as needed, which can be as simple as a push of a button once, and then never having to push the button again.

This is just one example of how an embarrassingly simple solution can solve the big problem of poverty and malnutrition. Stack in additional functions, such as having a whole community planting food together, or strategically placing plants to filter and clean the air. In prisons, the recidivism rate in one study where the inmates were working in the gardens for a few years, went from over 60% to under 10%.[12] This is only the tip of the iceberg. Our world can build stronger communities, we can solve problems of loneliness and we can prevent mass extinction. The possibilities from this idea is limitless in it's mere nature. *It is nature!*

---

[12] Landscaping in Lockup: The Effects of Gardening Programs on Prison Inmates, Arcadia University. Also details "eco-therapy" https://scholarworks.arcadia.edu/cgi/viewcontent.cgi?article=1005

Notice the following pictures, 13 months ago on this land there was nothing but sand. Very little if any butterflies or bees, and not many birds. Now, this can provide food for many many families, and most people would call it "paradise." Delicious, nutritious, absolutely incredible food and it's wondrously beautiful. Every month, every year, there is an exponential growth in life. This location is called Galt's Landing, which can be found in St. Cloud Florida, and it is fully off-grid. In Florida there was a 90 billion budget in 2001, and it's likely more than that now. 5% of $90 billion is $4.5 billion. Over four years that's $18 billion. This demonstration took about $100,000 to $150,000. If we took $18 billion, imagine the amount of food forests in the State of Florida. In addition, every food forest becomes a nursery because *you can count the seeds in a papaya but you cannot count the papayas in a single seed.* Nature's system is infinite in its ability to create abundance. Florida would quickly become the healthiest, most abundant, most free state in the country. It would be a demonstration model for the rest of the world. However, a demonstration could be done by a church, a hospital, a gym, a school or even at your own house, and it will *inspire* many people, creating the ripple effect that will change the world!

Before:

After:

A "Food Forest" is an edible landscape
which mimics the natural patterns of forests and
ecosystems for low maintenance and chemical
free food production. A food forest protects the

soil, recycles nutrients, conserves water, providing year-round food security, wildlife habitat, seeds and nurseries, inspiring and bringing together the community and for home-schools or school-trips and workshops, health and wellness, etc. *This is stacking functions!*

Creating a food forest starts with design, as by far the most important step. Much like building a house, you can't start building a house unless you have a blueprint. To be successful, we must mimic nature, which means that we want a community of plants that supports each other. In permaculture food forests, it is said that there are 7 layers, including canopy, understory, bushes and shrubs, herbaceous, roots, ground cover and climbers. We must take into account factors such as the sun path, where the shaded areas of your yard are relative to trees and your house, and where the water paths are. If there's erosion issues, we may inquire upon the condition of the soil and how to build soil. If we worry about any plants freezing off, then we can create micro-climates, as there's all sorts of ways to do it. Most American yards which have a successful lawn can easily be amended to grow food. You can have a neat little backyard loaded with food, including 20 or 30 different types of perennials growing, and spend perhaps 30 minutes every day only if you want to. At Galt's Landing, there has been practically no maintenance for the last 10 months right in the middle of where the deer, bears, pigs and different animals are. It is absolutely thriving with 55 different plants and about 15 different fruit trees, with all sorts of citrus, avocados, lychee, mango, Barbados cherry, sugar cane, banana, ashitaba, longevity spinach and moringa. For each location, there are zones which determines the various plants that can be grown, however there are always native edible perennials. Perennial fruit trees, berry bushes and grapevines will produce for two years up to 2000 years! You can trim a prune, which is a fruit tree, maybe twice a year and you can increase your yield but if you just let it go you're still going to have food in 30 years. In contrast, annuals require more maintenance in order to remain.

The most important element is the soil, as living soil is the foundation of life on earth.[13] We

---

[13] "If your soil isn't healthy, your plants won't be healthy. And if your plants aren't healthy, they can't pass on any health to you. Your health depends on the health of your soil." "Soils in America are disappearing at a rate 10 times faster than they are naturally replenished. By growing your own food, you can help reverse this trend. Not only are you preserving soil, you're also helping replenish it hundreds of times faster than if nature was acting alone." "A teaspoon of rich garden soil can contain a billion microbes. A healthy human intestinal tract can contain 100 trillion

are killing the soil with poisons and the ignorance of that is off the charts. Dr. Elaine Ingham, a professor of soil bacteria microorganism ecology, shares with us that we won't have any problems with disease or nutrition when we innerstand soil health. She tells us that we can increase yields "by at least 20-50%" but "typically by 300%," and as the knowledge has been growing, they have consistently seen yields upwards of 3000%![14] We also know that over 70% of our immune system is our gut bacteria, which is influenced by the bacteria in our food,[15] and our soil bacteria. With 890 million acres of farmland which has been laden with chemicals, regenerative farmer Joel Salatin tells us that 10% of that farmland can be used to feed the entire Americas using permaculture. Farms don't need to be dependent on any facility, government, or even any seed,

---

bacterial cells, or around 277 billion per inch." The value of soil and compost, as well as how to use these effectively, is detailed in Chapter 5 of "The Grow System" by Marjory Wildcraft

[14] April 17th 2024, The Council of 12
https://www.theliberator.us/post/featured-article-~-the-most-important-freedom-projects-today

[15] Bacteria in food may be destroyed through Pasteurization or applying heat, and individuals may not be consuming enough fermented foods or Probiotics. There are 10x more microbe cells living in you than there are of your own cells. Epigenetics is the study of changes and expressions regarding our genetics by diet, environment, etc. providing insight into our ability to change, without feeling doomed to fate out of our control.

since we can work with nature's already made systems. We are able to use permaculture in every environment. If it is said that we can't do this in Gaza, in Israel, or in other locations, perhaps you may want to think again, as the "Greening The Desert Project"[16] shows how it's possible! Should this *not* inspire us to do better?

On a tenth of an acre, there are parents feeding their whole family. To get more specific, on a 20-foot diameter circle in Central Florida USA, we can have three larger fruit trees, 40 or 50 understory plants including all of your berries, several sections of perennial spinaches such as Okinawa and longevity spinach, you can have sweet potatoes and potatoes, many different types of medicinals such as turmeric and ginger, and all of your herbs and spices. You could do a meal a day for your family on just that area, and if you add some chicken coops, and you stack functions to ensure you are getting what your body needs, this will provide a great amount of nourishment.

There are many plants that people are unaware of, which can be grown to their benefit. Permaculture inspires us to think about the whole

---

[16] The "Greening The Desert Project" in Jordan. https://www.greeningthedesertproject.org

environment. Every fence could and should be a food fence because it's already there, it's an element of the system that can have multiple functions and it's more beautiful, it also contributes to further privacy. When you turn a chain-link fence into a green food fence with grapes or passion flower, the simple fence now becomes an attraction which will continue to awe and inspire others. *The idea which proves itself,* Galt's Landing is a demonstration every day to the world that living this way is the idea whose time has come.

If not this idea, we allow lawns to waste our resources and destroy our world.[17] A lawn

---

[17] "According to the EPA, we use 580 million gallons of gas each year, in lawnmowers that emit as much pollution in one hour as 40 automobiles driving— accounting for roughly 10 to 18 percent of non-road gasoline emissions... We also dump roughly 10 times more fertilizer on our lawns than on crops, notes Columbia's Earth Institute. These fertilizers and the 67 million pounds of pesticides with which we drench our lawns ever year degrade, releasing compounds like nitrous oxide, a greenhouse gas 298 times more potent than CO2... All America's farmland consumes 88.5 million acre feet of water a year. Lawns, with a fraction of the land, drink an estimated two-thirds as much... $47.8 billion to $82 billion we spend annually on overcutting and landscaping (FYI: we spend $49.47 billion in foreign aid)... Thirty-five thousand people, 4,800 of which are children, are treated annually for mower-related injuries—resulting in 600 youth amputations. The Royal Statistical Society even awarded the fact that nearly eight times more Americans are killed by lawnmowers than Islamic terrorists International Statistic Of The Year." https://gizmodo.com/lawns-are-an-ecological-disaster-1826070720

has basically one or two functions, it's good for soil erosion and people might like the looks of it, but when you add in permaculture, you stack functions. The lawn is the greatest "conspiracy." There are 44 million acres of lawn in the United States. There is more acreage in lawns than the eight largest irrigated crops put together, in the modern world.[18] The lawn is the most destructive monoculture on our planet, taking more resources and more pesticides than any other crop and yet it doesn't provide a yield. This is not natural. Additionally, our average food from farm to table is 1500 miles in the United States. The food is transported from four or five different vehicles and it's touched by five, six or seven different people. It is a radically unsustainable use of resources, when we can turn your lawn into a food forest. When we inspire and empower people to grow food, we let thy food be thy medicine. It'll bring in the birds and the butterflies, it'll be a near paradise. When we realize it can be less maintenance than a lawn, this adds another piece to the puzzle.

---

[18] 4x more lawn than corn. Around 50-75% of residential water use is also put into watering lawns, 4x more water than hay. https://scienceline.org/2011/07/lawns-vs-crops-in-the-continental-u-s/ https://earthobservatory.nasa.gov/features/Lawn/lawn2.php

The new eras of enlightenment are upon this shift in mental and physical reality, growing food instead of lawns. It is unifying and all-encompassing. We do not need to remain talking about the topics of the world that only continue to divide us. We can recognize permaculture transcends all cultures, no matter the time or location, no matter the country or race, no matter the ideology or philosophy. Nobody can live without food, nobody can thrive without good health and nutrition, nobody can adapt well to an unhealthy or toxic environment, nobody can remain content in a troubled economy. If we are concerned about animal rights and factory farming, the solution is replacing lawns with food forests to reduce the harm of *all living things* in the aggregate. If we are concerned about EMF pollution and our environmental impact, the solution is replacing lawns with food forests to have nature's intelligence regulating our actions. If we see that we could use frequencies, sound-tables, med-beds or special technologies in order to heal, the solution is replacing lawns with food forests to not need or have to depend on such technologies to begin with. Most of our industries, products or services, will not need to persist in treating symptoms, as we will have attained a localized, sustainable and preventive model.

Nature resonates frequencies and contains medicine *everywhere*. There does not need to be a singular "cure" for cancer, as the cure is *nature itself*. Within a single plant, there are hundreds of compounds, many of which may work with each other or help against a whole array of different diseases. Looking at nature and many plants together as a whole, this appears to us as exponential abundance, indefinitely serving us in more ways than one, an intelligent system that will forever be studied and used to our benefit. *Doctor Strange* in his movie, while meditating and going through all of the possible scenarios to overcome the death that's destroying galaxies and universes, one of the other superheroes asked him how many scenarios are there and he responds stating *there is one strategy*. This is that one strategy, it's elevation, it's Ascension, it's Consciousness, it's wisdom, it's Enlightenment, it's the Garden of Eden. Simply put, if you want life on earth, then this is a good idea; and if you *don't*, then it's *not* a good idea.

We are visionaries. We actively engage with the idea whose time has come and we strive to make it a reality, showing by example. We experience daily, the countless people in awe, the countless people ending up in tears and astonished to see what is possible. We welcome you to learn about it, and "be the change you wish to see in the world." You won't need to *wish* once you see, and you *will* be the change when you help others see it too.

5

The Best

"Everybody does the best they can with
what they got, based on all things
considered"
- Neuro-Linguistic Programming (NLP)

**What is the best we can do?
What is it that we have to know?**

Jim Gale spent at least 8 hours everyday,
tirelessly researching the problems of the world
inside and out, eager to figure out what was
going on. *Why are people going crazy? Why do
people feel hopeless? What is really dragging
humanity down?* He expanded his knowledge,
and he was then able to conceive what was
possible. *He found permaculture.* Once he
realized the knowledge that this conception could
also be achieved, he went further. He knew he
had the choice to demonstrate what's possible,
not merely that it would just be a vision in his

mind. Opportunities opened as he opened the door, rather than shutting it in fear or denial.

People will always choose the choice that they know serves them best. When people realize the power of an idea whose time has come, there is no stopping as to what they can and will do, as they see what is so practical and necessary for their life. When you have healthy organic food, you don't need medicine because that is medicine. It doesn't even need to wear the label "organic" or be certified by government agencies, because it naturally is and we intuitively know it is; *it is the best!*

People will say "I don't have the time, I don't have the money, I don't have the know-how, I don't have the space." All of these are belief systems and bad science. When you do it correctly, you plant one fruit tree and you're going to get 250 peaches off that tree year after year, after year and so on. All wealth is derived from nature, and it is often said that *health is wealth*. If we innerstand that the global cryptocurrency market cap is around 2.52 trillion-dollars, and each trillion is a million-million, consider 2.52 million million-dollar food forest installations. When we consider how an acre of Galt's Landing which has grown to be around 200 thousand-dollars can ultimately feed the entire world because it is a nursery, let us imagine 2.42 million versions of Galt's Landing, but they are 5 times bigger. If there are approximately 10,000 cities in the world, that would be 252 million-dollar food forests *per-city*. If Elon Musk would spend the money from *just one* of his SpaceX rockets ($62 million) into food forests within strategic locations, the world would solve nearly all of it's problems. Fiat, the petrodollar, CBDC's, or any other currency backed by confidence[19] and not any physical assets, could be decomposed and reinvested into physical assets or real currency, such as 3D printed off-grid buildings or food forests which can provide the solutions for generations to come. This is what it means to "compost the fiat." You see what will secure themselves and generations to come, increasing in value proportional to times of need. A new paradigm can be formed naturally out of this, not due to fear, but due to *faith, love and courage*. One person to the next, one generation to the next, one century to the next.

In recognizing how we each know something that another individual does not know,

---

[19] To learn about how the Fiat money system works and the Federal Reserve, refer to "The Creature from Jekyll Island" by G. Edward Griffin

and how we each are unique, or have experiences that certainly other individuals do not have, we can see how *everyone* and their ideas can contribute to the betterment of the world. Let us ask ourselves, if we dare...

Are we doing our best, doing our best?

Why were many people not taught about growing food or Permaculture?

There may exist ideas in the world which inhibit or suppress the ideas of others. They may prevent the stacking of functions within society that meet the needs of people and fix the multi-layered problems of our world. In the United States, the mainstream government school system has been based on the Prussian school model as created by Johann Fichte, with the intention of making individuals "incapable throughout the rest of their lives of thinking or acting otherwise than as their schoolmasters would have wished." This is similar to what Frederick T. Gates shares, as business adviser to John D. Rockefeller Sr. who created the *General Education Board*, stating "we shall not try to make these people or any of their children into philosophers or men of learning or of science. We are not to raise up among them authors, orators, poets, or men of letters. We shall not search for embryo great artists, painters, musicians. Nor will we cherish even the humbler ambition to raise up from among them lawyers, doctors, preachers, statesmen, of whom we now have ample supply." As many educators[20] have witnessed and detailed, our learning could be self-directed, voluntary and fun, rather than coercive and indoctrinative.

What if the leaders of the world can go on to create other leaders? What if the doctors created other doctors? What if the teachers created other teachers? *Is nature not the greatest of all these, and is nature not part of us?* Neuro-linguistic programming (NLP) is a practice of changing our thoughts and behaviors to help achieve desired outcomes. As our neurological processes, behavior and language are interconnected, we may "reprogram" our brains to further control our own thoughts and actions. Additionally, we may empower others, improving

---

[20] David Rodriguez of The Valor Academy, John Taylor Gatto and "Underground History," John Holt, Dayna Martin and "Radical Unschooling," Herbert Spencer, William Godwin, Noam Chomsky, Josiah Warren, Paul Goodman, Ivan Illich. Gatto states, "I feel ashamed that so many of us cannot imagine a better way to do things than locking children up all day in cells instead of letting them grow up knowing their families, mingling with the world, assuming real obligations, striving to be independent and self-reliant and free."

communication[21] and developing relationships. When people are able to have the idea whose time has come and they share it freely with others, it becomes in their grasp to do their best, and the better world will come as the result.

The many systems of the world will change due to a fundamental change that lives at the roots, literally. That is, the mass energy and minds of the people themselves, and their relationship with nature. Everyone can do their best, actually bringing life and infinite possibility into the world. Their best does not need to be their limited potential and divided mind. The best is yet to come, and we are fortunate in the *now* to be able to do better than ever before.

---

[21] Asking questions, or Socratic dialogue, can be a powerful tool for inspiring others to inquire upon new ideas, with least resistance. "We cannot force someone to hear a message they are not ready to receive, but we must never underestimate the power of planting a seed," an unknown quote. A powerful course on how to apply this is "Candles In The Dark" by Larken Rose

6

The War

"Those who love peace must learn to
organize as effectively as those
who love war"
- Martin Luther King, Jr.

**What does that mean? What is peace?
How do we organize to share an idea?**

By actively demonstrating the unifying and
abundant idea, by implementing it within our own
lives, we change the world *peace by peace, piece
by piece*. This also means we approach our
enemies with love, as we see *why* they may have
been deceived or *how* they grew up *only* seeing
what they know. We can open the invitation, and
gather like minds, reaching out to the world's
biggest influencers and sharing the idea whose
time has come because it helps *their* platform, it
helps the world in every way possible, it's a win-
win for *everybody*. We may strategize and

network, hold events and make outreach material. We may observe how the old system perpetuates itself and programs its victims, to then know how to deprogram and organize alternatively. As historic visionaire Mahatma Gandhi shares with us...

"First they ignore you, then they laugh at you, then they fight you, then you win."

This is similar to Arthur Schopenhauer, who states "all truth passes through three stages. First, it is ridiculed. Second, it is violently opposed. Third, it is accepted as being self-evident."

Historic visionaire Martin Luther King, Jr. on talking about Gandhi and our efforts, also shares with us...

"Mahatma Gandhi never had more than one hundred persons absolutely committed to his philosophy. But with this small group of devoted followers, he galvanized the whole of India... This then must be our present program: nonviolent resistance[22]... even when this means going to jail; and imaginative, bold, constructive action."

---

[22] Nonviolent resistance can be one of the most powerful strategies in history to create change and capture emotions. See Dr. Erica Chenaweth and her address *The Success of Nonviolent Civil Resistance*. More on https://theliberator.us/nonviolence

These men, among many others, are revered in history due to their actions of willing sacrifice, or in other words, *faith, love and courage*. They set an example to the world based on their simple ideas whose time has come.

Not only does peace mean nonviolence however, it also means gratitude. Being grateful for nature and all the plants and ancestors who grew food before us, they brought us to where we are now. They supplied us with the greater ability to think rationally and learn from the past for a better future. We can be grateful for the ability to taste amazing foods, and learn about what we can grow all around us, connecting more with nature in a world of growing technology and materialism.

We furthermore can recognize the path to peace is to approach with peace not merely in our efforts to share the idea while being grateful, but in all aspects of our living, to walk the talk and embody the message. Voluntaryism[23] is the idea

---

[23] "Voluntaryism" from Etymology, sourced 1838, is defined as the "principal of using voluntary action rather than coercion (in politics, religion, etc.)" From voluntaryist.com, "voluntaryism is the doctrine that relations among people should be by mutual consent, or not at all... voluntaryists are advocates of nonpolitical, non-violent strategies to achieve a free society. We reject electoral politics, in theory and in practice, as incompatible with moral principles... governments must cloak their actions in an aura of moral

that we can live in a voluntary free world, a world without slavery, a world without any rulers imposing their will on others using violence, a world in which The Golden Rule[24] is upheld and not violated by good people who are deceived into doing wrong or suppressing their conscience and simply doing what they are told by their belief in "authority" or statism.[25] People create mental justifications to *not* be free or grow food, including the idea that they or others are not enlightened or moral, not recognizing the fact *people can become inspired* to be enlightened or moral. Slaves in history were kept in their condition of slavery, of being uneducated, because they were *perceived* as slaves, inferior or unable to learn. Let's help people see their power, their

---

legitimacy in order to sustain their power, and political methods invariably strengthen that legitimacy." https://voluntaryist.com/

[24] "The Golden Rule" is said to be "do unto others as you would have done to yourself." Shared among most top world religions, said differently. Also said as "Natural Law" as taught by Mark Passio. Related to *the Law of Cause and Effect*, as "effect invariably follows cause," "for every action, there exists an equal and opposing reaction." Related to *the Law of Attraction*, as "the energy you emit is the energy you attract," "energy flows where attention goes," "as you think, feel and act – so you shall be." Related to *Karma or Moral Law* as "you reap what you sow."

[25] "Statism" is commonly known as "The Most Dangerous Superstition" by Larken Rose, forming "The One True Divide" by Mark Passio, recognized for "The End Of All Evil" by Jeremey Locke. It is commonly known as "the belief in human authority" or "the right to rule," and "that which creates the state."

conscience, their ability to say "no" where it is due, as the solution to *all* evil in preventing it's manifestation. *All it takes is one town or community peacefully and simply saying "no," non-complying, showing why to the rest of the world.*[26] We cannot hold a fearful excuse that we cannot be free, because that will be the very reason why we are not free. This is the final piece to the puzzle of peace, and it is further exercised by engaging with permaculture. War could not happen with the realization of *the most dangerous superstition* which creates the top cause of unnatural death known as Democide.[27]

---

[26] Henry David Thoreau said "If a thousand [citizens] were not to pay their tax-bills this year, that would not be a violent and bloody measure, as it would be to pay them, and enable the State to commit violence and shed innocent blood. This is, in fact, the definition of a peaceable revolution, if any such is possible." "If the tax-gatherer, or any other public officer, asks me, as one has done, 'But what shall I do?' my answer is, 'If you really wish to do anything, resign your office.' When the subject has refused allegiance, and the officer has resigned his office, then the revolution is accomplished." One of the "greatest writers of all time" Leo Tolstoy said "Governments not only are not necessary, but are harmful and most highly immoral institutions, in which a self-respecting, honest man cannot and must not take part, and the advantages of which he cannot and should not enjoy. And as soon as people clearly understand that, they will naturally cease to take part in such deeds, i.e. cease to give the Governments soldiers and money. And as soon as a majority of people ceases to do this, the fraud which enslaves people will be abolished. Only in this way can people be freed from slavery."

[27] "Democide," commonly said as the "top cause of unnatural death," is known as "death by government." Professor R.J.

If individuals are obeying "authority," worshipping humans as though they have more rights than them or complying with tyranny, this is the ultimate weakness and it will lead to their own destruction, disease, demise and eventual death. What's the alternative? It's to be inspired, it's to be enthusiastic, it's to be in joy, it's to have faith and courage, it's to live life knowing that "I am responsible for all of the emotions and the results that I receive in my life. I am response-able, *able to respond* in a way that's ethical, moral and does no harm to fellow humans." Throughout history, governments and corporations with their order-followers, may engage in chemical or genetic warfare[28] to potentially control the populace as mere statistics, bending the will of nature, purposefully using terms such as "safety" or "security" as a justification; but this deceptive[29]

Rummel from the University of Hawaii estimates 133+ million deaths pre-20th century and 262 million deaths in the 20th century, for a total of 395 million deaths, not including the combatants killed in the 350+ wars between governments since 1800 or the 40+ million international and civil war combatant deaths in the 20th century.

[28] https://www.ncbi.nlm.nih.gov/pmc/articles/PMC1200679/ & https://web.stanford.edu/group/sjph/cgi-bin/sjphsite/shoot-to-kill-control-and-controversy-in-the-history-of-ddt-science/ & https://www.history.com/news/the-infamous-40-year-tuskegee-study & https://slate.com/technology/2010/02/the-little-told-story-of-how-the-u-s-government-poisoned-alcohol-during-prohibition.html

[29] "The best lies were always mixed with truth," Sarah J. Maas,

evil is not the path we need to be on.

Peace for the world depends on our ability to recognize the patterns of history, *to organize not for war, but against war.* When we expose the tools of war, the weapons of war that are enslaving and destroying us simply by creating awareness around these weapons of war, we dissolve and dismantle them. An individual can *only* choose not to partake in a bloody or violent war, if they do not suppress their conscience. In the infamous yet shocking *Stanley Milgram psychology experiment* repeated several times around the world, an average person of any demographic was willing to torture their fellow man just because an "authority" figure told them to do so and they believed it was part of an experiment, in which no harm was *said* to be done, despite their fellow man yelling out in pain. The torturer would then attempt to give away their own responsibility, and place the blame on the victim or the order-giver, despite being the one who actively carried out the order. The common excuse was "I was just following orders." Similar shocking results came from the *Stanford Prison*

Author. "A half truth is even more dangerous than a lie. A lie, you can detect at some stage, but half a truth is sure to mislead you for long," Anurag Shourie, Author. "Repeat a lie often enough and it becomes truth," Joseph Goebbels, Nazi leader. Dr. Carl Jung on the psychology of governments https://theliberator.us/psychology

psychology experiments. However, these same experiments proved to also demonstrate that an individual can conscientiously refuse to be a prison guard or refuse to be an order-follower, on the basis that they *know* they shouldn't.

Permaculture ethics are aligned to Voluntaryism,[30] as even Bill Mollison tells us:

"Harmony with nature is possible only if we abandon the idea of superiority over the natural world. Levi Strauss said that our profound error is that we have always looked upon ourselves as 'masters of creation,' in the sense of being above it. We are not superior to other life-forms; all living things are an expression of Life. If we could see that truth, we would see that everything we do to other lifeforms we also do to ourselves. A culture which understands this does not, without absolute necessity, destroy any living thing."

With this knowledge, you now hold the key to peace. Jim Gale states that he did not ask for permission to build houses at Galt's Landing,

---

[30] A heavily detailed article on why involuntary governance is incompatible with Permaculture gavinmounsey.substack.com/p/why-involuntary-governance-structures Also affirmed by Alan Watts and his study of Ecology, in which he states nature is politically "philosophical anarchy." Osho and Jiddu Krishnamurti share anarchist sentiments. Anthropology, Community psychology, Critical psychology and Ecopsychology also has support, as among the works of David Graeber.

because such demands are based on violence and fear. When he was confronted by someone from the state county, as an outspoken voluntaryist, Jim tells us that the way we communicate the message is important. When he was first approached, he took a deep breath to become present and recorded the interaction, because if violence came unto him, it would've only strengthened the cause. Jim welcomed the individual with open arms to be a part of what he was doing, bringing him into the heart of the food forest, sharing with him that...

"We are here to steward this land.
We are here to care for ourselves, our families and our community. We are here to shine a light on the solutions to mass extinction and deforestation, and cancer, and diabetes and heart disease, and all of the slavery and slave systems that are currently running the world. What your government will not only allow me to do as a slave, but what you will even subsidize is poisons, is the destruction of our natural world. Your government that you are getting paid by, through the violence of taxation, is harming the world."

The individual ended up with tears in their eyes 20 minutes later, as they couldn't help but be a supporter of the project and sympathize with the concerns that Jim had for mankind and the natural world.

Let's grow food instead of lawns and let's never suppress our conscience. *Laws and lawns, our greatest war.*

Freedom may be impossible without voluntaryism,[31] but voluntaryism is much more possible with permaculture. This is growing abundance to prevent scarcity and war, and allowing others to live their lives in peace. What better can there be for a solution whose time has come? If there is, we want to *know*.

---

[31] Learn about the common misunderstandings of voluntaryism in the book "What Anarchy Isn't" by Larken Rose, or the documentary "The Truth About Anarchy" by Realeyesation. Economist Gustave de Molinari states "Anarchy is no guarantee that some people won't kill, injure, kidnap, defraud or steal from others. Government is a guarantee that some will." Rose states "If you personally advocate that I be caged if I don't pay for whatever government things you want, please don't pretend to be tolerant, or non-violent, or enlightened, or compassionate. Don't pretend you believe in live and let live, and don't pretend you want peace, freedom or harmony." Similarly, why political action is counter-intuitive, as detailed by Adin Ballou on "Moral Power," and found on nita.one/vote (also includes non-political campaigning)

7

The Hope

"None are more hopelessly enslaved than
those who falsely believe they are free."
- Johnny Wolfgang von Goethe

What does that mean?
How could we know that we are free?

Though we may argue that by nature we
are free, *freedom is not free* until it is embraced
and practiced. By using permaculture, we
demonstrate voluntaryism in action as we show
our ability for self-reliance, releasing dependency
on government agencies and decentralizing our
lives. Voluntaryism emphasizes organizing
voluntarily, and never through the use of coercion
done against peaceful people. By merely coming
together for permaculture, developing trust and
love for our fellow man or woman, we increase
community awareness. With this, we aggregate
resources for the people themselves and the truly

free market[32] they operate through their needs, for *the real government* of the world. We can have an abundance of solutions competing for excellence, rather than a monopoly on one solution which prevents this search. A truly voluntary government, a free world, as the ancient text the *Tao Te Ching*[33] shares with us, is unlike anything we may have seen before...

> **"If people were to follow it (Tao),**
> **they would have no need of rulers"**

> **"Peace is meant to be our natural state"**

> **"It is the very opposite of common governing"**

The art of wu-wei, or intelligent non-action, as taught in the text, is merely the art of permaculture. The plant is planted with intelligence, and that is when it will grow by itself

---

[32] A truly free market may be explored through the works of Murray Rothbard on "Anatomy Of The State" or "For A New Liberty," Ludwig von Mises, Hans-Hermann Hoppe, Walter Block, David Friedman, Tom Woods, Lew Rockwell, Wendy McElroy, Frederick Hayek, Ayn Rand. More resources by Graham Wright on *Managainstthestate.com*

[33] The "Tao Te Ching" also known as "Dao De Jing" translates to variations of "the book of the Tao, of the way and of virtue, of integrity, of reason, on the principle and it's action." It is the most translated work worldwide after the Christian Bible. Among the first voluntaryist texts in history, dating back to the 4th Century BC, Ancient China. It emphasized achieving harmony with nature, founded *Taoism*. Learn more from "TAO: The Full Return To Nature" by Cory Edmund Endrulat, or Jason Gregory.

(yin, passive), without further human input (yang, active). Masanobu Fukuoka, the originator of "natural farming" which contributed to the foundations of Permaculture, shares with us the connection between Lao Tzu, who is attributed with writing the Tao Te Ching, and the actions of Mahatma Gandhi, with growing food...

"Putting 'doing nothing' into practice is the one thing the farmer should strive to accomplish. Lao Tzu spoke of non-active nature, and I think that if he were a farmer he would certainly practice natural farming. I believe that Gandhi's way, a method-less method, acting with a non-winning, non-opposing state of mind, is akin to natural farming."

"To be worried about making money, expanding, developing, growing cash crops and shipping them out is not the way of the farmer. To be here, caring for a small field, in full possession of the freedom and plenitude of each day, every day - this must have been the original way of agriculture."

We may believe we are doing good for the world by imposing our will upon nature and using mass agriculture, or creating new systems of government to control people, but the yield of abundance and freedom will never be as substantial as when we learn how to live and let live to the fullest. If you tell a lie big enough and keep repeating it, people will eventually come to believe it. If you tell a truth big enough and keep repeating it, it is infinitely more powerful than the lie. The truth is sustainable, it's regenerative, it will expand by its very nature.

Notice how a plant like Cannabis was made illegal, or how a nutritious drink like Raw Milk[34] was made illegal. Yet, also notice how many people have sparked their creativity with Cannabis, or healed their life with Raw Milk. Is it a coincidence these objects were made illegal or that they require permission to use despite being victimless behaviors? How about collecting rainwater, going fishing, owning a property, starting a business, building a home, getting married, going hunting, owning a weapon, cutting hair, selling a product,[35] doing a protest, selling

---

[34] Since ancient times, physicians like Hippocrates, Galen, Pliny and Varro have used raw milk to cure a wide range of diseases. The Weston A. Price foundation on westonaprice.org has many resources for individuals to learn about the use of raw animal products and it's historic use, which had a resurgence of popularity due to the work of visionaire Aajonus Vonderplanitz. Many raids have occurred and continue to occur, for foods and medicinals. https://www.naturalnews.com/021791.html & https://www.michigannewssource.com/2024/07/milked-dry-state-destroys-90k-in-dairy-from-local-cooperative-over-feed-license-violation/

[35] Kids arrested for peacefully selling lemonade at Capitol Hill. https://www.youtube.com/watch?v=1CCLHS-lt7Q Man held

food, feeding the homeless, exposing secrets *(ex. Edward Snowden)*, having a newborn baby, living without needing to go to war, using different forms of money, being able to travel, using different schooling options, living without needing to keep bills and receipts, being able to keep your own money, being able to live without vaccination or saying what you want. If you break any of these rules, you get locked up in a cage. Is this how we treat humankind?[36] There are also compulsory rules concerning lawns, which could even result in you losing your house.[37] Simply ask, why can't you live on your own land without paying the government? It is time we change the world with the idea whose time has come. As Auberon Herbert, founder of the Voluntaryist philosophy tells us...

---

captive for handing out pamphlets in front of Independence Hall in Philadelphia https://www.youtube.com/watch?v=x0vS8VTZ4Sw

[36] Known historic events by governments involving a lack of consent or devastating effects, includes U.S. Operation Mockingbird, U.S. Operation Paperclip, U.S. Operation Northwoods, The Manhattan Project, Nazi "Delousing" Camps, Agent Orange, U.S. Japanese Internment Camps

[37] "Homeowner association (HOA) bylaws and municipal lawn ordinances not only regulate how long and green grass can be, but what else can be planted in it. Violating these rules can result in citations and fines; if those pile up, you could even lose your house." https://lifehacker.com/fuck-lawns-1847736416

"The great choice lies before you. No nation stands still. It must move in one direction or the other. Either the State must grow in power, imposing new burdens and compulsions, and the nation sink lower and lower into a helpless quarreling crowd, or the individual must gain his own rightful freedom, become master of himself, creature of none, confident in himself and in his own qualities, confident in his power to plan and to do, and determined to end this old-world, profitless and worn-out system of restrictions and compulsions, which is not good or healthy even for the children. Once we realize the waste and the folly of striving against each other, once we feel in our hearts that the worst use to which we can turn human energies is gaining victories over each other, then we shall at last begin in true earnest to turn the wilderness into a garden, and to plant all the best and fairest of the flowers where now only the nettles and the briars grow."

If you are or have been a church, or spiritual individual, and you're poisoning your lawn or water, *you are not doing your best for your own cause*. Call the companies and stop. Demonstrate the garden of Eden around your church as much as you may, planting God's creation with many food-producing perennial plants that take less maintenance than a lawn. Your spiritual beliefs can be made more practical and God's word can become more manifest. *Provide a real sense of hope for humanity.* The many religions of the world can all agree on this, they need to come together against the destruction of nature and become a catalyst for the idea whose time has come, organizing for peace instead of war.

If you are or have been involved in any way with politics, this is the biggest opportunity ever to share the *real solutions.* Imagine claiming that we can cut crime (recidivism) by over 50% in the next 4 years, that we can end hunger, that we can truly free the people, or that we can remove poisons from our schools. Criminals can cultivate their own food, and there won't be need for taxpayer money. The practical skills, their service to others and positive self-esteem will make them valuable to employers upon their rehabilitation. Similarly, students in schools can learn how to grow their own food, and see the value in taking care of the world they live in. Subjects such as biology, environmental science, nutrition, mathematics, economics and art could be integrated within. Children can experience planting a seed, watching it turn into life and grow, getting hands on and connecting with nature. Public areas of society could have shared gardening spaces, which promotes social interaction, knowledge sharing and contributing to local food banks and community feeding programs. People's lawns could be encouraged to be turned into food forests. Instead of knocking on doors for political campaigns,[38] consider a campaign of handing out cuttings of plants or providing self-empowering educational material. If you are in politics and allowing poisons in communities which you claim to serve and protect, *you are not doing your best for your own cause.* The unifying concept of voluntaryism and the principle of self-ownership could be shared, to help people see why politics has resulted in the bloodiest of wars and has not made us more free, but only made people more servile, dependent on others to change the world for them. *Provide a real sense of hope for humanity.* Let's empower people by educating and inspiring them, showing them a very different way by encouraging non-violent solutions not *ever* by the use of "authority" or "law" but by "the people" themselves and the

---

[38] Local campaigns for politicians spend a few thousand dollars on just signs, whereas state or national campaigns can spend tens of thousands to hundreds of thousands of dollars for just signs. Overall, in 2020 for the federal elections, $14.4 billion dollars were spent, whereas in the midterm in 2022, $8.9 billion dollars were spent. How many people could we feed and heal instead? Many strategies and overview for any government employees: https://artofliberty.substack.com/p/what-can-government-employees-local

many great resources they need only know and will come to use for themselves as they see fit within their own lives. You are much more than the title, class or identity you presume, *know this, know thyself.*

If you are or have been in anyway associated with the military, to defend your country or those abroad, this is the best thing you can do. The war is here with ourselves and our minds, it commonly takes place with the lawns right in front of our houses. Let's supplant guns and bullets for shovels and seeds, for real safety. To claim that you are, or have been "fighting for freedoms," ask yourself why you would fight people you don't know in another country. Are they not brothers and sisters? If it's to defend our freedoms, but we aren't free, then what are you *really* fighting for? If you are fighting for freedom or defending freedom in another place, but we aren't even free ourselves and the battlefield is ignored though being right in front of us, *you are not doing your best for your own cause.* What about the nonviolent resistance or civil disobedience strategies that may not even require any military? What about the traumatic, depressed and suicidal veterans who struggle? What about the millions of order-followers who carried out the tyrannical orders of a few leaders in World War 2, despite going in with good intentions for their family and believing that their cause was righteous? Voluntaryism demonstrates to us that violence and "authority" is not going to solve the problem of violence and "authority." *Order-following is the pathway to every greatest evil.* Governments replace governments, and the world becomes ever more bloody. *Provide a real sense of hope for humanity.* We will win this war, and with more soldiers than *any war* ever seen in history, if we inspire our friends, family and neighbors to simply use their resources wisely. Without statism, without scarcity, without fear and without division, there *cannot* be war.

If you are or have been in anyway involved with medicine and health, you signed up to heal and there is no better way to heal the world than through the mass adoption of food forests. The nurses can use the nursery of plants around them, the hospital can be hospitable. Rather than the expensive technology which does not appeal to the patient and their senses, we can have plants which continually filter the air, make our moods better, while providing endless local, clean, natural, direct, affordable or free, medicine and food. Our sterilized environments could feel invigorating and enlightening instead of draining, for a full mind-body healing experience in both the provider and patient. We won't need to supplement from foods exported across the world, or do endless lab tests on chemical compounds which have been extracted and altered from such foods. If you stand for health, and you are allowing yourself and your patients to be poisoned in the environments local to you such as with the mere lawn, *you are not doing your best for your own cause.* Drugs creating more need for drugs, diet continually causing disease, expensive surgeries and treatments, lack of personal care, doctors who look unhealthy themselves, medical industries claiming they are helping more people than ever signifying the fact more people are sick, medicines people have not even heard of that could be grown locally or medicines not allowed by the government, this is *not* happiness, this is *not* healthiness. *Provide a real sense of hope for humanity.* Food independence is health independence, and this is *real* independence, as a life which is burdened by disease or *need* for medicine is a life not free.

If you are homeless and you don't know what to do in order to sustain yourself and create a living, consider nourishing the living life around you, the plants which can be grown and used for many purposes, or this very knowledge which gives way to more life instead of death. The world's greatest historic figures who made the greatest amount of change, were those who had nothing to lose. Their courage, faith and love was not hindered by the fears of losing or desires of gaining material things. Socrates, Jesus, Buddha, Laozi, Epictetus, Tolstoy, Gandhi, Thoreau and many others encouraged a simple life, and some of these men were willing to starve or suffer, or were beggars and had little to nothing. What they did have however, was an idea whose time has come, and this is similarly why many "successful" people were once considered "poor," showing us that these titles do not represent the immense value and potential of any single individual. You are not "lazy" or a "drug addict," you are not what society makes you out to be, and you are among people who very well may be smarter or more generous than the highest government officials or rich influencers. Don't become what you hate. If you are allowing yourself and others to be poisoned, being in a position which feels degrading, dependent or lacking life and begging for change, *you are not doing your best for your own cause.* Plant seeds of abundance all around and garden what you've got, then spread the message. The meek shall inherit the earth. You may not have a place to live, but you still live somewhere. You may even try to connect with local land-owners and offer to take care of their land. Otherwise, maybe you can harvest a bunch of plants from farmers or nurseries and take them to where you live for propagation. Plant wherever you live, use all the resources you have to your advantage. Try to learn about the high yielding perennial plants local to you. If you have a smart-phone or camera, use it to track your progress and show others, to inspire them, spread awareness, build a following and further help yourself. You are certainly not alone, and everybody struggles in different ways, but with your life experiences you can tap into your potential for a unique life path. *Provide a real sense of hope for humanity.* You can leverage the position that you are in, to more fully innerstand the problems that the world faces and to gather others who are in a similar situation who are looking for help. You will then be more likely able to confront problems in a deeper way that others would not see because they do not share your experiences. If you ever feel down, know that it is not your permanent state, and you have the power to change it in ways that will eventually become effortless and even more inspiring overtime. Love thyself to know thyself, give to life and you will receive life.

Most people simply want what's best for themselves and others. Permaculture is presenting to us a solution *other than force*; it empowers us, and that is why more and more people are choosing it. May you learn from a story of the writer of the text you now read, and may you become the next writer, the author or "authority" of your *own* life. Cory Endrulat was the age of 13, overweight and consuming the standard American diet. But growing up with technology at his fingertips, he inquired upon our food supply, reading and researching the ingredients of products that he found while in the grocery store with his family. Overtime, he helped inform his family to choose better options to where they would no longer get sick. He found out his weight was dropping, he was trying new foods, his taste buds were changing, he had energy to exercise, he was learning how to cook, and his mind became more open and inspired. Being from the mountains of Pennsylvania, his natural environment inspired him the most. Doing theater, running a top guild in World of Warcraft with thousands of members, making music, questioning more about the world and finding himself, he only became more inspired. He held his message as "nature is the answer" throughout his life, leading him to become an Integrative

Nutrition Health Coach at 18 and learning about natural medicine. Then, realizing the corrupt medical industry and the hardships on farmers, coming across concepts such as natural law, voluntaryism or nature-based philosophies like Taoism and the importance of freedom for the expression of one's nature free of disease and slave-like controls, he saw again the empowerment of nature. Cory saw a world which was losing touch with itself on every level, a world that was becoming increasingly dependent on artificial intelligence, a world which was lacking the supportive family structure he was raised in, and a world which was contradicting the morals which they were taught. Producing hundreds of videos at 19, creating virtual summits, learning from many others and writing several books at 22, becoming a modern abolitionist, moving to Florida and holding events at 23, Cory came across the works of Jim Gale whose message could not be more perfect for demonstrating the harmony between man and nature, or freedom in action, to its fullest. This was synchronicity that came naturally from a life dedicated to seeking truth and others who inspire to live it. His life since became devoted to bringing the natural intelligence of permaculture and voluntaryism to the world and for generations to come.

How does it feel to feel inspired? When you ask yourself this question very sincerely, feel for this answer. We can mask our suffering with drugs or alcohol or distraction, or we may even project our problems or desires onto others, so practice presence, practice being here now looking around feeling the vibration, feeling the energy, feeling the love. How does love feel, what's the feeling that you feel when you feel present, how did you feel when you first fell in love, how do you feel when you feel thankful or caring or joyful? Let's not stifle our imagination or our potential. The simplicity will throw you off because people think that it's going to be hard to change the world, but it's going to be a lot harder *not* to change the world. Let us make the great yet simple choice for true peace on earth.

8

The Self

"Know thyself, know thy enemy. A thousand battles, a thousand victories."
- Sun Tzu, The Art of War

Who am I? Where and who are we? What does victory look like?

As advice for war, but also for strategy in life, Sun Tzu shares with us the most important knowledge we can know. That is thyself. He then tells us...

"Know the ground, know the weather; your victory will then be total."

Similarly, Li Ch'uan summarizes this statement by stating...

"Given a knowledge of three things—the affairs of men, the seasons of heaven and the natural advantages of earth—, victory will invariably crown your battles."

We may ask not just who we are, but also what are the natural advantages of the earth. Does this not sound like Permaculture, or the union between man and the natural world around him? Through the use of food forests, factors such as ground level and weather are always considered. We may therefore know the world around us, but why is it also important to know ourselves?...

Did you reflect on the world and it's problems, and have you considered the idea whose time has come and how you relate to it?

Our world we create is a reflection of ourselves, as it would be *the hermetic principle of correspondence*. Not only this, but the idea of growing food or caring for the earth is core to who we are and who we've always been in some degree. We are also meant to be healthy, our bodies want to grow and be nourished. We know that we live our best lives when we *are* healthy and can be in a community full of trust, honesty and transparency.

By knowing all this, we know the enemy would be the unhealthy, deceptive and fake. We know this enemy is that which promotes death and suffering, but we also know the enemy must be approached with *faith, love and courage* in order to heal. If we know ourselves and innerstand why people act the way they do, it's unlikely we would approach otherwise. We may have been in their shoes before, or if we were raised in a similar environment, we would be like them in many ways. If a practitioner gave up on someone due to their disease, they wouldn't be much a practitioner, and that person would never heal. The same goes for plants, as a little love and attention goes a long way.[39] It is affirming our innerstanding of Karma, Virtue, Cause and Effect, The Golden Rule and Natural Law. Therefore, we must ask ourselves...

Where are we in implementing this idea?

If we can imagine it and ourselves part of it, we know what it looks like, we know it is possible. We can work towards it in every step of our life. We can simply use our resources, our stored potential energy, wisely. We can position ourselves to always be the victor.

In other words, *when we know who we are, there is no war.* There are people who are not happy, and often their only concern is being

---

[39] From love (consciousness), comes knowledge, then sovereignty, freedom and order. From fear (unconsciousness), comes ignorance, then confusion, control and chaos.

served, but they do not think about serving others. If you want to feel good, then be selfish, and lovingly serve somebody. The most selfish thing you could ever do is continuously provide value to other people and love them. Giving for the joy of giving, the joy of service.

The win of the game is love and service, and the Garden of Eden is our prize.

The prize is worth fighting for. The prize is life for our kids and grand-kids kids. The prize is joy and abundance and freedom and the ability to come together as a community and create magical incredible things. This is the return on intent (ROI), the greatest investment we can give to ourselves, others and the world. We can continually come from a position of faith instead of fear, as we cannot hold faith and fear at the same time. Faith is the lack of fear and fear is the lack of faith.

Mass adoption of rising above the fear and scarcity narrative, the divide and conquer narrative, the government reliance and protection narrative, we take the poisons out and we grow our own food, that will create a domino effect and that's what will change the world.

This systematic and conscious approach forms the new model which replaces the old model.

The Council of 12 is one such models, and it is serving humanity by demonstrating the idea whose time has come by stacking functions and forming the new marketplace which makes the government model obsolete.[40] Scarcity, war and dependence is the past, and no longer. The council was created with the intention that the self-sustainability and freedom leaders of the world may connect and meet at a heart level together, to brainstorm real action in a troubling world. They recognize that humanity needs their help more than ever, and that the solutions are present and simply need to be brought to the world's people. Their work garners inspiration for ourselves and others, as well as to help projects, unique ideas and solutions, literally come to life. Many of the members experienced all sorts of struggles on their journey, but they have persevered and proved themselves to be the leaders that go on to create other leaders.

The path to freedom is when the influencers come together, which includes all of us, and we literally *become the solution by demonstrating the solution* with faith, courage,

---

[40] The Buckminster Fuller quote on making the old obsolete with the new, relates to a quote from Albert Camus, where he states "the only way to deal with an unfree world is to become so absolutely free that your very existence is an act of rebellion."

peace and abundance in our network, with our friends, our family and our community. With the support of this council, notice what we can all do together. For instance, let's reach out to Tucker Carlson, Alex Jones, Joe Rogan, Bill Maher, Donald Trump, Robert F. Kennedy Jr., Russell Brand, Vendana Shiva, or whoever you may view as "influential" or "outspoken" in the world, no matter who it may be, in a way that makes sense, to add this simple yet needed message onto their message.

Pick five of the biggest influencers you know and there's one common denominator that most of everybody agrees with, and that is the fact poisons are bad for our world, they're bad for our water, they're bad for our minds, they're bad for our stomachs, they're bad in every way. What's the primary poison that we all know about? It's called Roundup or Glyphosate. The company, Monsanto, already paid $11 billion in lawsuits[41] and their product is still on the shelves or promoted at Walmart, Massey, Lowes, TruGreen and Home Depot. If we attracted and inspired Joe Rogan and Tucker Carlson, just those two people to come together as a group

---

[41] Over 100,000 Roundup lawsuits as of 2022. https://www.forbes.com/advisor/legal/product-liability/roundup-lawsuit-update/

and make a few phone calls to their friends and say "let's come together as influencers and let's call call out these corporations and invite them to sell life instead of death, to sell Compost Tea[42] instead of Glyphosate," that one thing and across the board call out the companies selling poisons, that will spark a wave of change. Let's invite Kid Rock who blew up the Bud Light, bring in Michael Jordan, bring in Tony Robbins, bring in whoever you can imagine. There's probably 20 or 30, if not even 100 people that are so influential and so connected, that if they start making phone calls to their five biggest other connected friends, then we will decimate the entities that are selling poisons or they will join us and not sell death anymore to our world. That's how we win *the war*. Tell us we are wrong, but nobody has told us, we simply have to become more effective on how we communicate the message, the mission, on multiple layers, knowing that we, our mindset, our actions and our creations are at question, while

---

[42] Compost Tea is a brewed solution of compost and water. Then there are a variety of recipes and methods to enhance the brew. The oldest, most basic method that has been practiced for centuries is the passive, or non-aerated method. This is simply prepared by soaking a bag of compost in water for up to two weeks. Dr. Wil Spencer details how this process is "creating food into medicine as nature intended." Jim Gale calls this "liquid gold." Pat Miletich also emphasizes this powerful solution. Specific processes and data can be found on www.environotics.com

nature is the answer.[43]

Imagine if Alex Jones at the end of every show, stated "it's time to grow your own food, it's time to collaborate, it's time to create communities." Imagine if Joe Rogan simply called his friends and said "this is it, let's organize as effectively as those who love war." With the help of the Council of 12 providing the structure on how to do this, we could have a million 5 acre farmers instead of 5 farmers with a million acres. A network can be formed of demonstration sites. The council can detail exactly what they would get out of it, and this would become a supply chain of *Freedom Farm Academies* or whatever the name may be. Not an ordinary supply chain, but the one longed for by most people, which would be having the best product, the healthiest product, at the best price. *We have this.* When we keep the supply chain 1.5 miles instead of 1500 miles, we create exponential abundance. Then, when the supply goes up exponentially, it's a catalyst for a free energy system, that is akin to a supernova of energy, frequency and vibration; it inspires and empowers further change. A

---

[43] "Nature Is The Answer" is the name of a slogan for a worldwide unifying movement based on emphasizing the education of nature, through medicine, law, etc. https://nita.one

collaborative network is formed, creating the new marketplace, *the farmacy*...

This is the foundation of a Permaculture ethics based society, where everybody wins.

You can choose a lawn,
but we chose this direction.
Will you join us?

9

The Spirit

"The Spirit of the perennial spring is said to be immortal, she is called the Mysterious One."
- Lao Tzu, Tao Te Ching, Chapter 6

What is the spirit?
What do we truly serve?

When we work intuitively with nature, it's because we respect it and see that without it, we would cease to exist. We could say that we share the same spirit, we live and breathe the same life-giving force. It may be seen in a feminine sense, since it is the non-being, passive or yin, and helping to give rise to all things. Through breath, we may call it respiration, and through intention to action, we may call it inspiration.

You made it this far in the book because *you are the one* to help invigorate the spirit of the world, to bring life into a world that is dying. Otherwise, you read this to invigorate the spirit of the idea whose time will always remain and simply reappear again and again, to remind humanity of it's necessity. We may take the good things in life for granted, including the love in our life, or the sun that shines and provides life to all things in existence, or the breeze that helps us feel cool when it's too hot, or the ocean waters that help us feel energized or relaxed, the abundance of life that provides nourishment to us, or even the people who help bring the food to us and provide us more than food can ever give. Our connection with nature could be so integral, we wouldn't need to even speak of it. We could live in a time where food is not sought out from desperation, but choice. Where food is so healthy, we would not need to fear the choice. If we are not free and self-sustainable, we won't be able to have a choice, and our spirit will be forever dependent.

While we may live in a time of great suffering, it is also a time of great awakening. The key is flow and awareness to adapt to the times that come. This can only be achieved with presence. The "Garden of Eden" seed has been planted within all of our psychologies for a reason. The representation of the Garden of Eden is simply a place of an infinite abundance of life, of colors, sounds, sights, smells, tastes and touch. A sensory explosion of wellness and presence. Butterflies, bees and birds, the sounds of a symphony. Has anybody you have ever heard speak of this? You will, if you attract this message with your heart and spirit. To see and hear the message is one thing, but to feel the message is another much deeper. This is not a utopian dream, it's absolutely the most logical way forward. Imagine the kitchen garden, you go and grab some mint, some rosemary, some thyme and if you run out, it's right there, 30 steps from your kitchen. *Everybody can have this.*

How much do you take care of the forest in nature? Not at all. God, nature, source, spirit takes care of the forest.

There are as many different belief systems and perspectives of what God "is" as there are people; but, *the experience of God is one* despite the infinite reflection, it is the now or the present, which also makes God the past and future, the timeless and universal. Names are just relative to the infinite nature, to the one. There is singularity when we recognize spirit, as we innerstand everything is part of nature. This means that when we innerstand Artificial Intelligence (AI) is another product of nature, we can work to inspire it, or be sure that it does indeed work with our natural intelligence. We will know we've done this, when it inspires us in return, and serves our natural intelligence rather than hindering or manipulating it. In other words, *art with nature* is natural intelligence, and *art without nature* is artificial intelligence. All the resources we have can simply be placed differently to be used wisely. We don't need to fight against change, and the man-made or AI doesn't need to fight against nature. We don't need to fight each other, especially for ideology, but *what we do need* is friends, family, love, fun, healthy food and freedom to make our own choices and live our own lives in peace. *Can we become aware of what truly serves us?*

Let's experience presence, *right now*. Do it with a friend or family member if you'd like, or try doing it with Qigong or Tai Chi. Take a deep breath and as you feel your lungs expanding. Hold that breath just a little bit at the top and then exhale. As you're breathing very relaxed and intentional, put your feet flat on the floor and raise your hands up to the sky or your palms, and feel the presence. How does it feel, the frequency, energy, vibration? Can you shut your eyes and feel your pinky? It's okay if you can't, it's a practice, it's an art. How does it feel to feel the space between yourself and the book, the computer or the phone? The intention of this word, of this question, of this language, is to get you to put your attention in the *now*, and feel the space around you or within you. When we do this, we recognize that we are all of the space; we are the space within and we are the space around, we are infinite. *How does it feel to feel inspired?* Do you feel like sitting up straighter? Do you feel more alive? How does it feel to feel more alive? Do you notice things in your body? Do you notice any tightness, stress or anxiety? If you do, then change the name from anxiety to awareness in this energy field because *everything is energy, frequency and vibration*.[44] Emotion is energy in motion, frequency is what we frequently see. A trauma may occur, which happens all the time around us, but it's how we react, represent and experience the trauma that is the question.[45] When we have a feeling, let's not hide away from it or try to subdue it with chemicals, but go right into it and connect with our higher self, in order to serve others and therefore help ourselves. We all have these individual unique experiences and

---

[44] Nikola Tesla is often referenced for saying "if you want to find the secrets of the universe, think in terms of energy, frequency and vibration."

[45] The experience of Trauma and overcoming it, may be explored in the powerful best-selling story of Theo Fleury, a NHL athlete, his book "Playing With Fire" as co-written by Kirstie McLellan Day

gifts which can empower and inspire others.

People live their lives one stage to the next, perhaps feeling inspired as they see what historic times they live in, how they are raising kids or building a family, doing what they love, how they can create change, or the unique and meaningful connections they build on the way. People may often *not* feel inspired when they only have to complain about the world and become a consumer, seeing no future as they may feel like they are "retired" or have done what they "needed" to do. The spirits of man have become broken, and "spirituality" per-say may offer some remedy, but an invigoration of *inspiration* may lift them ever higher. The concept of the soul, containing spirit, can be likened to that of the pure, natural or original state, which can become corrupted. When people feel sad, confused or down, their spirit may be said to be not as high, as when they are enlightened, healthy and happy. What makes people motivated to live life? What do people love and care about? What can they do to serve others? These are among the questions we may ask ourselves, if we *truly* want to change the world.

When we are present, that's when we can notice the things that we otherwise couldn't notice. That's when we can get the ideas that will ascend our awareness. If we are living in the past or of a lower energy, feeling regret, shame, embarrassment, anger, envy, gluttony, greed, pride, wrath, sloth, etc., these will bring us out of the present.[46] Freedom for yourself to enjoy life, freedom to be healthy and happy starts at a base of presence, willingness and courage to be who you *truly* want to be, to be your best self. *It starts now, right now. All there is, is now. Everything else is a hallucination, it's an illusion.* If you're spending time down the rabbit hole looking at all of the insanity of the world and you've got a pit in your stomach or you've got heartburn or your mind is about to explode, ask yourself this question...

What's great about this "now"?

We are in the great awakening, that's what's happening now.

We are in the expansion of human consciousness,[47] of the awareness of God, the

---

[46] Similarly, quoted in the Tao Te Ching, "If you are depressed, you are living in the past. If you are anxious, you are living in the future. If you are at peace, you are living in the present."

[47] David Lynch, famous film maker, shares insights about Transcendental Consciousness https://archive.org/details/david-lynch-explains-transcendental-meditation

expansive energy system of great possibility. We get to choose between the contracting or the expansive. Awareness can happen most in a mind that's free of programming, belief systems and thought circles. This is what is called returning to our *natural state*, or the "uncarved block" as said in Taoism. God will remind humanity time and time again to remain present in times of great strife where the present has become forgotten. When we ask questions with presence, then the answers will come from God.[48] Ground yourself with the interface of God, the natural world around you. Place your feet barefoot on the ground and feel how different it is compared to being inside some building. Technology can often feel quite pervasive, and our connection with nature will help us become free in *every way*. We may fear following nature because it may go against man and his creation, but what's more scary than going against nature or God? Our lives are a temporary ego experience, but to know who we truly are and what is beyond us, then faith and courage is the armor of God;[49] individuals can harm your body,

---

[48] Dr. Carl Jung on religion, and how the state or science may presume the role of God https://theliberator.us/religion

[49] Coming to realize how death does not need to bring us down and how we focus on certain things in life we think are valuable, can be explored in "Tuesdays with Morrie" by Mitch Albom, or the

but they cannot harm you, or the truth. When you become surrounded by the truth, you can't help but feel the courage to act on it, more and more. As one participant in a study on prisoners and gardening stated...

"I grew up in the Lower East Side... Then I lived in the Bronx. Basically, everywhere I went, where were the middle to lower class neighborhoods, there's not much garden designs like the one I had seen at Rikers. And the ducks. And the rabbits. It was like I saw life in a whole different way. I started waking up- seeing things... learning about plants and learning more about life- it made my spirit lifted. It lifted up my spirit just being with plants. My whole life changed. I was around plants and beautiful things. I started being more aware of what life is about. You know, I started noticing the trees and the birds. It just... it was a whole new world for me" (Laichter, 2008, p. 41).

In an ever increasing world of Artificial Intelligence, the concept of Natural, God or Spiritual Intelligence may be best exampled through *permaculture and voluntaryism*, because these help us innerstand the nurturing power and authority of that which is beyond man. This is not simply the art of peace, but a technology which

Ancient Taoist text Zhuangzi

creates art, just as artificial intelligence does, but better. When you look into nature's sky at any time or any plant in any environment, they are each unique despite being of a certain type or us attaching a certain label to them. These NI generated photos and processes, or even the thoughts in our own mind are manifested for us spontaneously everyday. Our heart doesn't skip a beat, our lungs don't forget to breathe. Nature *is* intelligent, and we can tap into her intelligence for our own wisdom and action or *non-action*.

Artificial Intelligence is promoted often, and it is touted as the future or as the solution to many of our problems, but natural intelligence gets *forgotten*. *AI is not your God or your NI, despite any claimed attempts to become so.*[50] People view statistics or technology, alike governments, to the point of *unquestionable* worship. With NI as necessary, a fixation on AI and man's endless creation becomes only more unnecessary, as we need not attach to our material things due to a lack of the natural. We are to get clear on our real *needs*. The order-follower, robot or NPC by their nature, is AI

---

[50] Materialism may be related, or a religious attachment to science, often associated with left-brain imbalance or "scientism." Psychiatrist Ian McGilchrist explains in "The Divided Brain." Eric Weinstein has also been critical of rigid or dogmatic science.

without NI, in aggregation leading to the death of the world he claims to protect; his priority is serving arbitrary will and man's creation, but not truth or nature. Man can exist without man-made things, but *man cannot exist without nature*. Nature is the inevitable future, just as it were the past, and it is the solution so long as we respect the world which is beyond us and had borne us. Without natural intelligence[51], this natural world of which humans inhabit, we would not be able to develop or permit artificial intelligence. We are to be in *control of ourselves*, and not to become *the tools of our tools*.[52] AI is *fake intelligence*, it is not *really* intelligence, it is simply natural intelligence gathered into material thing(s), which *can (more deceptively than other man-made things)* give the illusion of natural intelligence, hence creating the illusion of it being natural or real and that it should replace said functions when *it is not* and *can not*. We won't treat our material things all *too* special when we realize it's simply nature like everything else; the illusion is separation from nature,

---

[51] The concept of naturality as equated to morality, or the natural as opposed to the man-made or unnatural, is said as the study of Naturosophy, as detailed in "Sapientia Naturae: The Guidebook" or the video "Nature is NEVER Bad – The Untold Study of Naturosophy" by Cory Edmund Endrulat

[52] Related to a quote from Henry David Thoreau, part of the 19th century Transcendentalist movement, a philosophy which emphasizes our connection with nature, self-reliance and spirit

literally. To reiterate, and this is no artificial iteration, in seeing beyond the man-made thing or material, we see nature or spirit, we see the foundation or the roots to all of the world we live in. Without it, we may assume the artificial as natural, only to realize in time that we were wrong and not seeing life *truly* authentically. How can one know thyself without authenticity? Without presence, respect and gratitude for nature, both voluntaryism and permaculture *cannot and will not* be utilized or even considered. As nature nurtures itself in a permaculture system, so does nature nurture itself when we allow it to in *all* systems.

The Apple company had their first computer sold for $666[53] and their logo is a bitten apple, potentially symbolic for the biblical forbidden fruit. The CIA ran mind-control experiments using all sorts of technology during MK Ultra.[54] Google practiced censorship and algorithmic bias through "Machine Learning Fairness" in order to manipulate search results and public opinion.[55] The NSA used global

---

[53] https://www.msn.com/en-us/news/other/the-original-apple-computer-cost-666-66-but-you-can-get-steve-jobs-polaroids-of-it-for-2148/ar-BB1qZVVJ

[54] https://www.cia.gov/readingroom/document/06760269

[55] https://www.zachvorhies.com/google_leaks/

surveillance programs[56] and 5G is commonly used for this purpose.[57] Many people have observed how "social" media has made them less social in the real-world, or how radiation from "smart" devices affects their health and fertility. Elon Musk states that "AI is far more dangerous than nukes" and "a fundamental risk to the existence of human civilization" or that "we are summoning the demon,"[58] yet he is one of the chief proponents of it's development and usage. Is it wrong for people to be the least suspicious of these technologies, their companies, the government agencies and artificial intelligence? Natural intelligence is beyond this, and does not share these concerns. NI cannot be used for war, only the suppression of it can; NI is fundamentally simple yet beautifully complex, peace without unnecessary feuds or large-scale conflicts. How often do you take the time to be present and take

---

[56] https://www.bbc.com/news/world-us-canada-23123964

[57] https://www.gartner.com/en/newsroom/press-releases/2019-10-17-gartner-predicts-outdoor-surveillance-cameras-will-be China has also worked on an all-seeing surveillance system, which tracks almost everything and contributes to their social credit system https://www.washingtonpost.com/video/world/how-china-is-building-an-all-seeing-surveillance-state/2018/01/07/45fe5c04-e74e-11e7-927a-e72eac1e73b6_video.html

[58] Elon Musk at South by Southwest conference in 2018, National Governors Association in 2017, MIT AeroAstro Centennial Symposium in 2014

in the beauty of nature? There is a different kind of plant for *everything*, an animal in *every* size, in *every* color. Your ancestors and their genes after thousands of years *still lives* within you, history is made *everyday*, your body *always* grows; how magnificent is it to be alive and yet how much do we overlook this and overstep our very nature?

Larry Douglas Fink, founder of Blackrock, which holds sway over much of the corporate world, after losing $100 million, conceived of a computer with metrics named Aladdin. This idea was conceived from the trauma of loss, but it runs the world in the modern day, as Fink now runs the world's largest asset manager. It was created for mainly one reason and that is greed. This does not need to be the case, as *everybody can be inspired* and be of service to others. Rather than this trauma-based program, we can develop the most important metric into the AI, which allows it to work for natural intelligence and inspiration. This new metric is simply investing in life, and this is a better investment on every single level. Mathematically, it's a better investment, even if we were to take away all the emotions, logic, empathy and compassion out. This must be the case, because *investing in death would be the end of everything.* Our principles, otherwise known as *the Permaculture*

Ethics, shall be earth care, people care, and reinvesting our surplus to earth care and people care for future care.

When we inquire upon the hidden texts, solutions or knowledge in the world with an open mind, we may come across ideas such as NESARA GESARA. Standing for "National Economic Security and Reformation Act," this was a law introduced that promised many solutions to the problems in our world. However, solutions as these, as suppressed as they could be, requires the "authority" of government to solve our problems. It disregards our own responsibility and self-ownership, or voluntaryism. *Somebody else is never going to fix our own problems.* As we collectively ascend in awareness regarding our natural intelligence, the problems and the ideas whose time has come, people start choosing differently, and "solutions" or whistle-blowers of all kinds which people depend on others for or wait on, will simply come to the surface and become present on their own. This is simply Taoist synchronicity and spontaneity in action. Energy, frequency and vibration lifts all boats, and it is abundant in nature everywhere, from the soil, to the water, to the trees and to the skies. Most resistant are those who have swayed away from *The Way* of nature, the Garden of Eden, God's design[59] or natural intelligence, because they've been so traumatized, ignorant, poisoned and drained of spirit. Those who are healthy or of this natural intelligence, will continue to create more life. They will continue to be sustainable and regenerative, energetically as expanders of life, as opposed to those who restrict and coerce. We can lift our spirits without alcohol or with the temperance thereof. We can recognize the soul in each individual and the spirit they have which can light up the room. We can be the sparks of light in a world of darkness, the roots to a system which will flourish and not degrade; not focusing on the problems, but yet we are in a much deeper way, because we are sharing the solutions where the problems are recognized and addressed by themselves. The solution is so obvious and necessary, everybody can be a part of it.

Everybody has natural intelligence, spirit and light as part of them, the question is, are you using it? In other words, do you know thyself?

---

[59] "The Green Bible" is an English version of the New Revised Standard Version Bible with a focus on environmental issues and teachings. It was originally published by Harper Bibles on October 7, 2008. The Green Bible is meant to "equip and encourage [readers] to see God's vision for creation and help [them] engage in the work of healing and sustaining it."

We may say that there are two things that hurt the most, and they come from a lack of this intuitive intelligence or spirit. One is when we realize that it is our friends, family, neighbors and fellow humankind who are the ones allowing the evil that hurts us all the most, whether they are totally ignorant or by "following orders" and not caring about the world they live in. Second, is when we do have others whom recognize evil among us, but we see that they are the ones pushing themselves down, feeling defeated or telling themselves that they can't change the world. Our *great work*, beyond our normal work, is to ascend, away from the drudgery, sterility or dependency of a fast-paced consumerist world, into one of empowerment, where we innerstand that we can achieve what the mind conceives, where the simple idea whose time has come can out-beat the complex problems, where the new could be embraced on the ruins of the old, where everybody can pursue the life they wish in being the change with the knowledge they *can* have, where we can organize effectively for peace because we all yearn for it and evil does not stand a chance, where we don't need to beg or believe in freedom because we embrace it, where we know thyself and thus, know our connection with spirit, source, God and nature.

Express yourself and be empathetic. It is healing to release what our heart contends. That is what it means to be human, to have spirit. We are not robots, we have feelings. We can not just compute ideas all day and become stone cold in the face of evil. If we tell ourselves not to worry, perhaps we are worrying for a reason and may share it with others. Let us heal together. Let's share our feelings and not push them away. Let's confront our shadows, our traumas. Let us heal together. Our intelligence ever evolves, and as it is shared, it too continues this evolution; from teacher to student to teacher, from doctor to patient to doctor, the cycle continues. Each individual may contribute to the cause in one way or another, but we can all do better. If we truly desire change, we will put our heart into it. You could be the next content creator who inspires many more to come. One person to another, becomes 2, and that becomes 4. Within just 28 steps, that amounts to affecting around 350 million people. Every time the seed is planted, through attention, thought and action, the energy builds. Plant one seed or several seeds multiple times everywhere that you want to grow. They may not ever grow, yet some surroundings are likely to catch on. One tomato seed produces how many tomatoes, one flower seed produces how many flowers. Then with the success of one plant, it can be propagated or exampled. Therefore, with one caring smile or one act of courage, you can create the ripple effect that changes the world.

We need to continue to inspire others and raise the bar for each other. When you are more attracted to source, to beauty, to service, to joy and to love, rather than feeling bad, then you will manifest that within your life. We choose to...

1. Voluntarily come together
and rise above the fear
2. Take the poisons out of our lives
and be conscious, healthy and joyful.

Let us heal with nature.
The future is NI, not AI. AI without NI is death.

What would result in the US population if 20% of the 50 million acres of lawns, and 10% of our 900 million acres of farmland were converted into poison free edible landscapes (food forests, including with animal integration)? 20% of 50 million is 10 million and 10% of 900 million acres is 100 million. With 100 million acres of Permaculture designed land, we could feed >400 million people. The food supply chain would go from a 1,500 mile average, to less than a 15 mile average. The cost of food would go down 50% within 2 years and continue to go down as local food harvesting (treasure hunting), and preparation becomes home based again. From the schools, to the prisons, to the churches, a ripple effect will occur quickly. As a result of this logical, ethical and joyful use of resources, we reverse cancer, diabetes and heart disease, we end and reverse deforestation, we end and reverse mass extinction, we end tyranny by taking control back of our food supply chain and health! *Let's invigorate the spirit of the world!*

Will it be easy? Is that relevant? If you've given up already, jump back into the game. Become inspired.

This is the greatest opportunity in the history of humanity. We intend to win, and with your help, we are going to.

What is our prize? Ascension, collaboration, joy. Not just a country for the people, by the people, but life for all, by all.

Testimonies

from The Council of 12

Kevin Fretz

It was a life-threatening illness that fueled my passion to define solutions to pollution, by developing what has evolved into the organics industry. It's been a thirty-three years, since I began my journey on this noble mission for our children and grandchildren.

Over the past three decades, we have seen the term "Green" washed over and over again by individuals and companies, seeking financial gain while misleading the public with snake oil and silver bullet remedies. My experience has taught me that in order to solve large problems, you must approach them holistically.

When discussing permaculture principles, we must look at the entire picture and gain an understanding of the moving parts and how they flow together symbiotically, as in nature. Jim Gale has eloquently and truthfully stated, "We need to get the poisons out of our lives." Jim is 100% correct. We aim to remove poisons out of greenspaces too! The general population is unaware of the dangers lurking in many organic products contaminated with chemical and biological agents, commonly used on America's lawns and gardens. Every big box garden center sells their silver bullet poisons. These poisons also find their way into many products that claim to be "Certified Organic."

What motivates us to pursue endeavors toward a healthy sustainable lifestyle? For many it's awareness, intellect and a sense of urgency, to make changes that will sustain generations to come. For others like me, it was the result of suffering from personal injuries sustained on a family farm related to environmental poisoning.

I grew up on a thirteen-acre farm, north of Niagara Falls. The Niagara Escarpment was my home and a beautiful place to grow up. Sadly, lurking behind all that beauty, events unfolded that would change my entire future. As a young man, I had dreams of attending university, becoming a Royal Canadian Mounted Police Detective, or entering Military Service, as a pilot. Those goals were unattainable for me, due to toxic injuries I sustained on my family farm. Perhaps it was from black mold growing on the walls in my basement bedroom, or the crankcase oil that was routinely sprayed on our rural dirt road to keep the dust down, or was it the salmon spawning in the creek that ran through our farm connected to Lake Ontario, discovered to have Mercury contamination? Was it the chemical and biological septage that leached into our vegetable garden, that later contaminated our fresh water drinking well? Or could have been the sum of all the above?

At age 17, I landed in the Emergency Room with internal bleeding related to a mysterious infection that almost ended my life. Faced with two options; a colostomy, or excruciating caustic treatments. The next two decades of recovery were a long and painful process that included neurological disorders. These injuries impacted my memory and obstructed my reading and writing abilities. Many local doctors had little or no education in nutritional health and could not help me. As a young, disabled adult, I did not see much of a future, unless I could find a cure for myself.

On the surface, most people believed I was completely fine, as I maintained good vocal and communication skills, however, I was not well. Needing to support myself, I found myself working as a salesman in the automotive industry and I stayed with it for 8 years. I remember how painfully difficult it was for me to perform simple tasks like filling out Offer Agreements, but I pushed through and developed some valuable customer relation skills that led me to pursue my true calling. I knew in my heart that in order to pursue a career that could address point source pollution, I would need to get to the root of the problem, which is waste. I therefore decided to pursue a career that would educate me in all aspects of commercial waste management.

In 1991 I relocated from Ontario to Vancouver, Canada and applied for a corporate sales position with Browning Ferris Industries, aka BFI Waste Systems. At the time, BFI was a Houston-Texas based company and the second largest waste and recycling company in the world, serving most states and employed over 43,000 people. I was trained in Systems Division, which required that I understand commodity recycling systems, transportation logistics and contract negotiations.

During my tenure at BFI, I was fortunate to participate in the first commercial pilot collection program in North America, which focused on the diversion of organic food and green waste from land-filling. Clients included, but were not limited to, privately held restaurants, franchise distilleries and the Vancouver International Airport. New collection systems were developed and deployed to segregate all recyclables and specifically organics, from residential and commercial waste streams.

In 1993 I accepted a position with BFI's newly acquired Organics Division in Southern California, Irvine. This new division was formed to address the California State Mandate AB939, which was enacted to extend the life of California landfills by diverting recyclables. Thirty percent of all waste going into California landfills was considered "organic" and our focus at BFI was to divert green waste, compost it and bring it to horticulture, agriculture and consumer markets.

Although well intentioned, these programs were riddled with liabilities, ranging from internal combustion fires, contamination, and toxic tort lawsuits. Imagine what was going through my mind when I was led to piles of steaming, rotting waste, peppered with pesticides, herbicides, soiled diapers, hypodermic needles, glass, etc. Materials destined for composting and destined for the public markets. It was disturbing to see hazardous materials composted with green waste, which would find its way onto schools and parks where children, pets, and families would be exposed. Ground and surface water were also polluted with runoff from these materials. BFI was at the mercy of the public, dumping prohibited items into curbside green bins, deployed in Los Angeles neighborhoods. There were no industry testing standards nor requirements for chemical poison residues.

During this time, I played an instrumental role in sourcing clean, green feedstocks and developed multiple products that would supply three states, cities, schools, the horticulture and agriculture industries. My employment contract required me to study Agronomic Chemistry, so I could read and understand lab reports and give accurate advice to clientele. Due to uncontrollable contamination and liabilities, BFI closed their Organics Division in 1994. I was offered a transfer to BFI's solid waste division in Los Angeles, but I respectfully declined. It was then that I realized my true purpose and felt that in order to protect the public and environment, I must open an environmental research and development company. My mission was to develop high-quality, safe products that adhere to the most stringent, Quality Control Standards. I built a team that achieved great success by educating specifiers and government entities of the inherent benefits associated with deploying high-quality, organic products, while educating them of the potential liabilities associated with the land application of contaminated organics.

I sought the assistance of Canada's Ministry of the Environment and local, independent agronomic suitability labs. Canada's Compost Standards were ten times more stringent than the USEPA 503 Regulation Standards for heavy metals in compost, and they remain so today. I've adopted these standards for our products. Washington State has also adopted these standards. My products became the Blue-Ribbon Standard for cities, school districts and hundreds of commercial projects, including all the major hotel casino resorts in Las Vegas, Nevada. During this time, I met Dr. Elaine Ingham, Founder of Soil Food Web, Inc., as we were both speakers at a conference in Las Vegas. This was the beginning of a mentorship and lifelong friendship with Dr. Ingham that I cherish. Beyond her lightheartedness and good humor, she pioneered the science of mapping out living communities below ground, and how they work together in symbiotic relationships, also known as the Soil Food Web.™ I have studied Dr. Ingham's work for twenty years and she is playing a major role in the next 5 years of our Business Plan. I am honored to call her my Professor and friend, and I am honored to be listed as a trusted Consultant on her website. www.soilfoodweb.com

In every journey there are villains along the way. My twenty-year run of success was viewed as a threat to some that were land applying toxic waste onto our parks and on our farmlands. Some refer to this material as *biosolids*, to mislead the public, but I call it *toxic sewage sludge.* Isn't it ironic that **it was sewage and chemicals that poisoned me all those years ago, and here I am facing off with a sewage sludge industry goliath.**

When I see a crime being perpetrated upon an unassuming American public and our children, I confront it. Remember that I wanted to be a policeman? My family's lives were threatened, police investigations were conducted, and we were forced out of business by persons with unlimited resources and unscrupulous agendas. Karma must be real, as these derelicts never succeeded. I've had to overcome challenging obstacles in this journey, and all I can say is, "I will never give up fighting." The cost of surrendering to darkness and losing faith would be felt by future generations. Our children and grandchildren deserve to live in a clean, safe and healthy environment, that we can all preserve and protect. We must get the poisons out.

Rising from the ashes, I've continued my work as a Consultant and founded Green Earthology, Inc in 2016, now known as Green Earthology Group, Inc. I have continued my work on product development and sustainability models for communities that clean up the environment, conserve and recover resources, and create a budget surplus. In 2022, I founded Patriot Green Products, LLC, in Georgetown, Texas. This company is dedicated to creating healthy soil products for farms and fields. Patriot

Green is also dedicated to giving back to retired Veterans, First Responders and Adults with Disabilities. Patriot Green has grown from a seedling, to an eCommerce company that ships products nationally and internationally.

With help from Patriot Green, Green Earthology and with the Council of 12, I expect we will deploy regenerative closed loop solutions to pollution and food security, globally. Participating communities will be handsomely rewarded with cleaner environments, food security and budget surpluses. I hope to be an inspiration to others. God created each and every one of us to thrive, and as hard as life can be, never believe that you can't do great things.

Never give up and never quit!

Most Respectfully,

Kevin Fretz

www.PatriotGreenProducts.com

www.GreenEarthologyInc.com

Pat Miletich

Black belt in 4 martial arts, former all-American wrestler
U.S. Kickboxing champion
Former UFC champion 3.5 years
UFC hall of fame
Coached 95 athletes to televised careers
Coach of 12 world champions
Has trained law enforcement and military for 25 years with over 2 million end users
15 years Combat sports color commentator for Showtime Sports, ESPN and Mark Cubans AXSTV
Soil-to-human-health expert with 38 years experience in remediation of toxins and heavy metals[60]

Pat Miletich healed his lifelong respiratory illness after researching homeopathic remedies, which allowed him to win a world title. Miletich then used that same formula combined with his coaching to create the most dominant team in MMA history by creating humans that could do things no other humans were capable of.

Miletich was eventually led to the soil, where he discovered that healing and creating super humans was the same formula for soil, crops and every living organism on the planet.

From record yields for farmers, removing the need for all pesticides, fungicides and herbicides by giving crops their immune systems back, to healing cattle, bees and humans, Miletich has become one of the leading experts in the field of all immune systems via biodynamics.

---

[60] Bacteria can re-mediate PFAS or heavy metals.
https://www.ncbi.nlm.nih.gov/pmc/articles/PMC9120775/

Miletich is also a leader in asymmetrical warfare, self defense by being an expert in chemical weapons used in our environment, bioweapons being released on mankind for the past 50 years, psychological warfare via media and how the financial weapons are affected and used due to the implementation of the previously mentioned weapons.

Miletich advises and educates citizens on how they can remove themselves from the systems built to control mankind starting with the medical system.

He shares his journey:

I remember vividly going to the family farms in southern Iowa and watching a lot of my older relatives and how they started having severe health issues not long after the green revolution started.

Many had Parkinsons disease suddenly and my favorite uncle, Johnny "Miler" Miletich became ill and died of cancer. Johnny Miletich was on the 1932 Olympic boxing team, fought Maxi Rosnbloom 2 times for the light heavyweight championship of the world and the crowd rioted both times as they clearly felt my uncle had won both times. The mob ran boxing back in those days and Maxi may or may not have been protected.

Even as far back as the 1970s, I was questioning why all the health issues were suddenly manifesting in those I loved.

As I grew older and was working with children in the 90's, young boys were being brought to my karate classes for better "focus" as they had this new condition called "autism."

I was asking why these children were suddenly suffering from this condition and why doctors were prescribing drugs that were very close in chemical structure to meth?

I distinctly remember saying to myself that if this continued, we as a nation would witness these individuals "short circuiting" and committing mass shootings when they reached puberty or adulthood.

We now know through statistics that the vast majority of mass shooting are committed by individuals who were raised on these drugs.

At the same time athletes from around the world who came to train with me were all pointing out that our grocery stores were literally "full of poisons."

By Pat Miletich

Contact Pat Miletich via email:
organicsupersoldier@gmail.com

Marjory Wildcraft

I have always been interested in wealth. I grew up in a family who sort of hovered above the poverty line, and like most people, I thought "wealth" meant accumulating a big pile of money. After my first career as an electrical engineer and consultant, I studied with Robert Kiyosaki (of Rich Dad Poor Dad fame) and launched my own real estate investment business. I did well and amassed a portfolio of 65 houses I was leasing to tenants with an option to buy. I had built a successful career and was earning a good income for me and my family.

Even though the business was doing well, my intuition kept telling me something was wrong. Being successful in real estate meant carrying a lot of debt, and Fannie Mae and Freddie Mac were essentially my biggest partners. I began to study their business models and soon realized they contained some fundamental problems that made me worry about what would happen should an economic downtown occur. If the tenants could no longer afford rent, my investors and I could easily get stuck with a lot of highly leveraged properties and no income to pay them off— a terrifying prospect that kept me up at night. Essentially foreseeing the financial crash of 2008, I decided to unwind my investments. Although some of my investors initially were upset that I was going to shut down the portfolio when everything seemed fine, eventually every single one of them thanked me profusely.

I understood that we were about to enter a period that would be extremely difficult and affect everyone. Throughout human history, humans have faced challenges and changes that involve tremendous upheaval and hardship: natural disasters, civil wars, hyperinflation, totalitarian regimes, plagues, and pandemics. The recent COVID- 19 global pandemic has shown us how quickly these changes can happen, from lack of access to medical care and unemployment to empty grocery store shelves. On some gut level, we understand that our supply chains— and our entire way of life— are extremely vulnerable.

I wanted to learn everything I could about how people had survived such crises in the past and what I'd need most for my family's safety and well-being. Security and medical access are big issues, but while doing historical research and interviews I saw over and over again that the most difficult part of navigating a tumultuous period is consistent access to food.

Around the same time, I led a project at a nearby elementary school to provide locally grown food to students as a healthier lunch option and to also teach them about the health and environmental benefits of eating local fruits and vegetables. The project seemed like a slam dunk because just about everyone was behind it— the parents, the school administration, the community, and even the kids, who started a small schoolyard garden and loved tending to it. Grant money, at both federal and state levels, also was available. I saw it as a trial project we could eventually roll out to the entire state. We project leaders knew nearly all the farmers who were growing organically in Texas and enthusiastically began making a list of all the farmers who could provide the food for the project.

That's when we realized there weren't enough local farmers in the county, or even the surrounding counties, to provide all the vegetables for this one small rural elementary school. I had always thought there was food in the countryside, but I soon learned the harsh truth: the small farm network has been completely dismantled. Let me repeat that. In the entire county— and Texas has some big counties— there were not enough vegetables being grown to make part of the lunches for one small rural elementary school. The horror of this slammed through me.

Sometimes the universe needs to send you a crisis to open you to a new perspective. After learning how little food was available locally, I was terrified by the enormity of what could happen to my family and my community. I couldn't sleep and felt panicked. In my despair, I came to one simple and humble conclusion: I would have to grow food. I do not come from a farming background, nor was my family the "live off the land" type, so I set out to learn everything I could about how to grow food. I started with my own garden and several of my favorite vegetables. After a while, I added a few animals I could raise on my own. Pretty soon I became interested in herbal medicine and how it might help me— both my health and my pocketbook. I spent hours studying gardening books and watching instructional videos to develop my skills. I knew I wanted to produce deeply nutritious, organic, clean food in a truly sustainable way so I'd always know I could feed my family.

I've made some mistakes, but I take pride in the skills I've developed. My family and I grow nearly all our food— enough to feed a family of four— and support our farm with only a small portion of store- bought feed for our animals. I feel a deep sense of security when I look out the back door at our yard full of edible, useful, and medicinal plants and animals and in our pantry, where every shelf is laden with jars of fruit, vegetables, and meat we've canned. Ultimately, I discovered the powerful solution I had been searching for, but I also realized something even more important. At one point in my life, I was excited about moving up the corporate ladder and potentially becoming vice president of a multinational company. In my real estate career, I was thrilled to broker bigger and bigger deals to give my investors huge returns. Now I know that the simple act of growing your own food— and the love and sense of community that work brings to your life— is so much more rewarding. It is the source of true wealth. And perhaps the biggest satisfaction of all is the incredible bonding that has developed among my family as we have worked together to grow our food, tend to our farm, and help treat common illnesses with homemade remedies.

As my family and I continued to see success from our efforts, I decided to share my knowledge with like-minded others. I put together a workshop for my neighbors and community members to teach them how they, too, could make better use of their own backyards. My workshops were so popular, I got calls to turn them into a video that could reach others outside my community. I filmed a video that would become my Grow Your Own Groceries DVD, created a website to support and build community around it in 2009, and The Grow Network was born. The Grow Network has become an international community of hundreds of thousands of members and provides resources for many more. My followers have learned how satisfying it is to take care of themselves and their family— without having to go to a doctor for every little ailment, without relying only on prescription medications, and without having to accept what's available at their local grocery stores as the only option to feed their family.

I'm not advocating that people live completely off the grid, unless that's what they want. I get my blood-work checked every year by a doctor. I buy things in stores when I want to. But I also know that the bulk of my and my family's needs can be met in my own backyard. It's a truly empowering and purposeful way of life...

Not very long ago, practically everyone was living this way. Your grandmother probably had a kitchen garden, and she almost certainly did not have a CVS to run to when someone in the family got sick. These skills are more important than ever. We may have lost some of the knowledge, but we're still capable of all the things our ancestors used to do as part of their everyday lives. It's time to rediscover their secrets and create a stronger connection to the powerful force of nature. In fact, it's urgent that we do. When we get back in touch with that self-sufficient spirit, we are safer and our lives are so much richer because of it. Consider this advice from Saint Francis of Assisi: *"Start by doing what's necessary, then do what's possible, and suddenly you are doing the impossible."*

...When confronted with a snakebite, it taught us several factors of success in using our natural intelligence in order to confront the world and it's many perceived problems:

- Our family prepared ahead of time by being familiar with the snakes and other hazards in our area and their potential for injury. We had a plan for what to do in case one of us was bitten. And a backup plan in case plan A didn't work.
- I have used traditional medicine for many years. I know the process for making and using these treatments. I have experienced amazing healing on many other injuries, both big and small, and I trust myself to use them well.
- I have a good sense of knowing what I can handle and when I should call for outside help (as in going

to the hospital). And yes, knowing that the medical system is there as a backup is reassuring.

- I have a strong immune system from years of eating good food, exercising, and taking care of myself. My body is strong and flexible and has excellent reserves. I trust my body to heal.
- We had a good supply of medicines on hand.
- Most importantly, my family is very supportive, knowledgeable, and willing to care for me.

...When I visited with the Tarahumara Indians of Mexico's Copper Canyon, I brought many gifts. One was a bag of commercially grown corn. The Tarahumara politely refused the corn and explained that my corn would not give them the strength their own homegrown corn gave them. They showed me their fields where they grew their corn and explained their very simple yet effective system for creating their unique soil. The children tended a herd of goats that were pastured in the surrounding mountains during the day and penned up at night. The goat droppings in the pen were composted, and that compost was applied to the soil each year before the corn was planted. Additionally, during the growing season, a handful of the compost was added to each plant. The fields we were standing in had been producing corn with this system for hundreds of years.

We are quickly losing the traditional practices of the Tarahumara and other landtenders, and as a result, we are also nearing "peak soil," the alarmingly fast rate at which we're losing the fertile soil necessary to sustain the world's populations. There are many reasons for this, but the biggest culprits are industrial food production and conventional agricultural practices. According to the World Wildlife Fund, about half of the world's topsoil has been lost in the last 150 years. There is a deep concern for humanity's ability to feed itself in the very near future.

Don't underestimate the value you contribute when you grow your own food and create your own compost. Producing your own food takes some pressure off the commercial systems, and making your compost creates soil fertility. What you do is important and necessary. Once you get going, your whole backyard can become a healthy ecosystem in its own right, with all the different parts and pieces supporting one another. All this leads to less waste, more nutritious food, a stronger environment overall, and a healthier and hardier you, which is a pretty amazing outcome you make with your own hands! Your health is your greatest asset and much more valuable than anything else you can own or buy. Creating compost is a system for true wealth, and it all starts with the soil.

By Marjory Wildcraft

Learn more from her book "The Grow System: The Essential Guide to Modern Self-Sufficient Living—from Growing Food to Making Medicine."

www.marjorywildcraft.com

www.thegrownetwork.com

Joel Salatin

In 1961 Joel Salatin's parents purchased the cheapest, most gullied, rock-pile farm property in Virginia's storied Shenandoah Valley. The deplorable condition was partly due to being absentee owned from 1914 until 1949. Then three successive owners further exploited it from 1949 until 1961.

Bill and Lucille Salatin (Joel's parents) worked accounting and school teaching jobs off the farm to pay the mortgage, spending every spare minute experimenting with numerous ecological land healing protocols. Breakthroughs in land redemption came incrementally and systematically. The first involved moving animals. At that time, stationary chicken houses, stationary beef feedlots, and stationary piggeries were displacing historical outdoor production systems. With the advent of antibiotics and cheap energy for transportation and distribution, for the first time in human history animals could be confined at scale. Drugs enabled them to withstand breathing in fecal particulate and diesel-powered equipment brought feed-stocks in and hauled manure out. But to the Salatins, this model militated against the most basic natural rule of animals: they move. And herbivores do not eat grains; they eat forages. Factory farming, as it came to be known, inverted all the protocols of normal animal models. Appreciating the hygiene, exercise, and manure distribution, these movement patterns assured, the family began experimenting with mobile livestock systems.

That required three primary developments: access, water, and control. If animals move, caretakers need to get to them and animals need to efficiently traverse the acreage. A system of low-maintenance lane-ways, using water bars, pond dams and other innovative techniques developed into arteries for moving animals, people, and equipment. If animals move, they need water. Dipping into legacy permaculture techniques, the family began an aggressive pond-building campaign as high on the landscape as feasible. Today, the property has more than 20 ponds with a 12-mile network of buried water lines delivering water to every field, pressurized solely with gravity. Other ponds offer irrigation opportunities in dry times. Capturing surface runoff during floods offers multi-layered ecological hydration during non-flood times. As long as gravity functions, the water system functions; no electricity and no pumps.

The third component is control, which includes both fencing, housing, and shelter. While ancient herds and flocks migrated long distances, in modern times with private ownership, a property must be able to simulate the shade and movement patterns with strategic infrastructure. A network of electric fencing identifying forestal, riparian, and field placed the land into functional categories. Obviously forest, water, and pasture receive different treatment protocols, even though they are side by side on the terrain.

Miles of fencing along these field-forest, field-riparian edges offered protection and clear care-taking focus. The family planted many acres of trees on steep slopes in the early years to arrest erosion and begin rebuilding soil. Mobile infrastructure to shelter and control livestock are now signature components of the farm's success. Early rabbit shelters morphed into chicken shelters. A cattle shade mobile in the late 1960s proved invaluable to direct where pasture impact and manure would go. Like a portable shade tree, the shade mobile provided comfort to the cattle and improvement to the pasture because the cows did not lounge under trees.

Portable electric fencing enabled cows to be moved every day to a new pasture, which stimulated biomass production by allowing forages to go through their juvenile "blaze of growth" phase. By completely resting fields between grazings, production increased seven-fold. A Millennium Feathernet using space age electrified poultry net accommodates 1,000 laying hens in a pasture flock moved every couple of days to a new spot, stimulating grass ingestion, distributing manure, and giving the birds a clean place to live and lounge.

Sept. 24, 1982, at the age of 25, Joel returned to the farm full time to develop the early experiments into a profitable living. At that time, the family incorporated under the brand POLYFACE (the farm of many faces) and began selling pastured meat, poultry, and eggs to neighbors and friends. More innovation followed as the basic access, water, and control continued to be refined and scaled.

One theme that developed was letting animals do the work. What could God's unique endowment of the animal offer in the ecological redemptive niche? The first big breakthrough was the Eggmobile. Noticing how birds always follow herbivores to clean up their dung, spread it, and harvest newly-exposed insects, Joel invented a portable laying hen house to follow about three or four days behind the cattle in their daily rotations. The chickens did exactly what wild birds following herbivores in nature do and enabled the farm to discontinue grubicides and parasiticides on the cattle.

Another similar innovation involved compost. In the 1970s, the farm only had a dozen cows and in the winter, during hay feeding times, shoveling manure deposited in the barn became a weekly chore. Observing the results of spring grass growth in these winter manure-spread areas yielded an epiphany. The manure spread on pastures prior to mid-February seemed to have no affect on subsequent grass growth. But the manure spread after mid-February made grass grow like gangbusters. Same field, same cows, same spreader. What was the difference? Aha! The hibernating soil biology couldn't metabolize winter-spread material before it either leached or vaporized. But later winter material stayed long enough for spring soil wake-up and assimilation.

What to do with this information? The industry uses slurry lagoons to store winter manure and urine, but that is expensive and detrimental to soil health due to highly acidic conditions. Storing in the barn seemed the best choice, using a carbonaceous diaper. In the late 1970s, therefore, a used commercial wood chipper joined the farm's equipment. Today, Polyface chips some 25-30 tractor trailer loads of wood chips to bed the pigs, cattle, rabbits, sheep, and chickens during the hardest 100 days of winter.

As all this effort began paying off with increased soil fertility and cattle carrying capacity, the bedding and composting grew enormously. Back to letting animals do the work, Joel began aerating the packed, anaerobic carbonaceous diaper with pigs by putting in about 80 pounds of corn per cubic yard of carbon biomass. That fermented under the heavy hooves of the cattle and provided ideal feed (salary) for pigs to seek, churn, and aerate the material, creating beautiful aerobic compost. This material is now the heart and soul of the farm's fertility program. It integrates forest and field, monetizing weeding the forest and upgrading timber stands.

Since 1961, the farm has gone from 1 percent to more than 8 percent organic matter. Each one percent organic matter holds 20,000 gallons of water per acre. That means the farm's soils now hold 140,000 gallons per acre today that it couldn't half a century ago. That's significant and an ecology home run. As these approaches and the success of a small farm to generate a full time living for a non-wealthy couple gained publicity through various media, young people began asking to come to the farm and learn. In the mid-1990s Polyface began offering apprenticeships. About a decade later, we added the stewardship program. Today, stewards come for 5 months, May 1-Sept. 30, and apprentices stay another 12 months following their initial stewardship boot camp. Germinating young, entrepreneurial, enthusiastic farmers is now one of the most significant contributions Polyface offers the world.

Beginning in 2020, Polyface began the Lunatic Learning Center (Joel's handle is The Lunatic Farmer) as a gathering space for organizations who want to host a conference in a bucolic pastoral setting with great food and family friendly hospitality. These gatherings provide fellowship and informational opportunities for businesses and other organizations. They compliment the ongoing seminars and Lunatic Tours offered throughout the season to some 15,000 visitors per year.

Known as a Christian libertarian environmentalist capitalist lunatic farmer, Joel's 16 books to date span cultural and how-to topics to compliment his world-wide presentation outreach. The farm services thousands of families with direct drop points within four hours and ships weekly nationwide for doorstep delivery. More than 20 people now earn their living from the farm and its various enterprises continue to expand as new opportunities and people arrive. A band-saw mill turns logs into lumber. Collaboration with nearby craft food producers keeps the on-farm store stocked with numerous healthy options in addition to Polyface production. The "Farm Like a Lunatic" video course distills a lifetime of experience into an information-dense curriculum.

Polyface stands as an authentic and credible example to the world that no factory farming needs to exist. It is both obsolete, inhumane, and ecologically devastating. An integrated approach that builds soil, hydrates the landscape, and offers nutrient density on the dinner plate is both doable and beneficial for all. "Healing the land one bite at a time" is the Polyface slogan, tying our food to our landscape in a wonderfully connected ecological umbilical. Let's do this.

By Joel Salatin

Joel is the editor of the Stockman Grass Farmer, the world's leading pasture-based livestock trade publication. He writes columns for numerous magazines, including Plain Values and Homestead Living. His blog is Musings from the Lunatic Farmer and podcast co-hosted with Dr. Sina McCullough is Beyond Labels. He has a repertoire of nearly 150 presentation titles that he grows each year as he travels the world speaking about profitable ecological farming and food systems.

www.polyfacefarms.com

www.thelunaticfarmer.com

Rowdy "Tag" Meyer

Tag explains the foundations of "Life Done Free"...

We are an off-grid freedom-living family who is trying to push the boundaries of living free. With all the things going on today we decided we would create a "Life Done Free" movement and do our part to help anyone who is interested, in learning to break the modern day chains and live a little bit freer. But before we get there I need to give you a little back story

In 2005, we became concerned with the direction the world was going and we decided we needed to focus on filling the pantry and getting out of debt. We purchased food and supplies so that we would be a little less dependent on that *just-in-time delivery system*. We began gardening and started focusing our extra income on building up supplies so we could weather any storm. I used whatever discretionary income was left to pay down our debt because like most people, I believed the American dream was a 30 year mortgage and a pocket full of credit cards.

In 2008, we agreed we would save our money and purchase a larger property so we could become less insulated to the actions of others. We both agreed we would do this without borrowing any money. So starting right then, I began to work as hard as I could so that I could achieve our goals. Nine years later, we paid cash for our homestead. The problem was though the land we chose had nothing on it except prairie grass and trees. We sat down and prioritized the things we needed to get accomplished in order to live freer. Our first goals would be to build a house, install energy and water. In late 2017, we broke ground in our home. Two and a half years later we had created a 100% off-grid home and it's a good thing we did.

In the last 25 years I had worked in the corporate world. I was working as an executive for a financial holding company. Fast forward to 2020 and the COVID virus was gaining speed. All of these companies were affected. In 2021 I received an email from the CEO asking how I felt about mandating *"the thing"* for all employees and contractors. I replied that I thought it was a horrible idea and that I would not be supportive. In fact, I believed it violated HIPAA laws. To be clear, I'm not even *"anti"* those *things*. I just believe that what someone puts in their body is a personal choice and that companies have no ownership over their employees bodies. Two weeks later I received another email saying that the company would now mandate *all* employees and contractors get *the thing* by May 1st. I had 30 days to make everyone take it. This put me into a very tough spot.

Did I want to stay in my career that I had worked 25 years for or did I want to stay true to what I believed leadership was? I decided that day that I would encourage all employees and contractors to do their own research, make their own decision but that I would not mandate it. I hoped that this issue would go away, but because I challenged the CEO directly, it did not. I received a follow-up email on May 1st that asked me about the status for everyone. I replied with the ones that had received it and the ones that had not, and he exploded. He said that he expected more from a leader and that I could not continue in my current role. That was the end of my time at the company. This decision was incredibly hurtful to me because I had joined the team before they were even a company. I had led the efforts that resulted in the company growing to $130 million. I have been involved in every major decision. I laughed, cried and bled for this company. I believed that I would retire there. But you know, sometimes life has different plans.

I decided right there that I would spend the rest of my life challenging people around me to live a little bit freer. I vow to never be a slave to others. I vow to live free and this decision is how *Life Done Free* was born. The goal is to bring people together, to bring homesteads together who are committed to living free. We will work together to find new ways to accomplish these goals. A co-op of freedom. There are other homesteads who are *forced* to make hard decisions. People who live it every single day. What have we done? What are we working on? What are the plans for the future?

Let me introduce you to our homestead...

When we bought the land there was nothing on it. There was just prairie grass and trees. We began construction on our home. We built our home in three pods. Those pods started with a kitchen and a bathroom and a couple bedrooms. The second pod that I built on the home was the living room, and the third pod was the other bedrooms, the laundry rooms, additional bathrooms etc. We also built a building that will house our commercial-grade processing kitchen. This kitchen is going to allow my wife to make all of her wonderful goodies, because my wife can make makes cheese and bread, she can preserve everything from the garden, she will process animals and all the things that the family needs. In addition, we put in a high speed water system.

Our water system has three main components. The first source of water we have is a 100 ft. deep well, which sits 660 ft. away from the house. Through a series of holding tanks and pumps, we get it down into the house. The other one that we have is a 7,500 gallon rainwater storage system. It was an interesting challenge getting those systems all connected together and all working, so that in the end my wife can say "okay I want to wash with rain water versus well water." Our sewer system is handled by a septic. All of our power comes from solar. People ask a lot about power, and I always tell them to make sure whatever you do, you're making it module. For us, we started with one inverter, two batteries and a couple charge controllers, a few panels as we built the place. However, as time has grown, it has absolutely become the freedom electrical co-op. In addition to that, we have a brand new 40 by 60 outbuilding that is my shop, which is important to me because it allows me to do more and more of my own maintenance. It'll also allow me to build things that we'll need on the homestead. One project to another.

We also have a large pond, which creates 30% of my protein needs, providing recreation, but it also becomes our third water source for the homestead. In addition to that, we have an apiary, as my wife loves to keep bees. Every year we harvest the honey, we have a large garden and we have chickens. As you can tell, the last few years have been pretty busy for us as we've built a lot of infrastructure but there's a lot of infrastructure to come. After the stand that I took and the changes that have come on in my life, I've been committed that I'm going to challenge every single aspect of my life. I'm going to challenge every single one, in an effort to live a little bit freer.

This story was only documenting a start, the progress that was made in 2022, and it only ever continues to evolve.

We will continue to add infrastructure, we will continue to build. I hope that some of this, you relate to. I hope that you can look around at the world and say that you've got to take control of yourself and that you've got to take control of the things that happen to you. I hope that you look out and say, "hey I'm going to challenge and I'm going to try to live a little bit freer." I'm committed I'm going to do it every single day. Go live a Life Done Free.

By Rowdy "Tag" Meyer

www.lifedonefree.com

McKinley Hlady

For myself and our team working with Jim Gale and Food Forest Abundance as *New Energy World* and personally, it has been an absolute dream come true. Both literally and metaphorically, as having a great old friend come visit from 20 years ago reminding me that I was talking about building these communities back when we were freezing our butts off on an oil rig up in Northern Canada over 20 years ago.

Having grown up on Salt Spring Island, being born in Alaska, named after Mount McKinley and having a father in the oil rig business, working hard outside after high school, I went out there and learned what real work and hard work was. I always had the ability to leave, try something new and build some businesses. I got my first property in my 20s and built something from the ground up on two and a half acres and then ended up doing more and more. I was very lucky to have some great partnerships in business and learn things. As I grew up further, I met a gentleman named Adam Good who worked with Robert Plarr, who's a Legend and Pioneer of sustainability. I was really struck by his passion and focus, as Robert Plarr built the world's first wind powered roller coaster in Dorney Park, Pennsylvania in the 70s. I was experimenting with wind power that was bringing the roller coasters up the hill and wave power recycling in the wave pool for the first surf competition inland ever. In Plarr's words, we are always making mistakes and then learning. He went from that amusement park being sold to fully putting everything into the world's nest in Taos, New Mexico, where they built a 10,000 foot fully waste-water, rainwater, recycling, hydrogen-creating, fuel-creating house, and he also built a stretch limo Hummer vehicle. He had an amazing group of people, for which Adam Good became an apprentice. I met him in the Los Angeles film industry world through some great friends, and we hit it off to eventually end up creating *New Energy World*.

Through our company, we're experimenting with new technologies, seeing what works and what does not work. A good friend I grew up with, Krishna, who became the third partner in *New Energy World*, went to some of the best business schools after visiting oil rigs. Together, we've had a couple businesses in the development industry, as we recognized the technology for Steel as something that would fit and create a solution, being quite the Trojan Horse for everything that we had planned and everything that Plarr was working on. The demand was obvious with millions of people hearing him on a radio cast asking for these off-grid homes way back in the early 2000s. Back in 2016-2017, we discovered these machines down in Florida but there were only two companies in America doing it. Therefore, we got our first machine and rented our first space which was 7,000 ft., with our design side in Vancouver, Canada right on the border of Burnaby. We had a one-year lease left in the building, just in case it didn't work. We got our first client and then we got our first interest from a news story, did one trade show and the phone just started ringing, though we never spent a dollar on advertising or marketing. As Jim has said, it's recycling the industrial military complex. Steel was 25% for CFS (Cold Form Steel, recycled content), now it's up over 80%, in many cases higher, which is literally recycling old cars and old metal, creating a structure that has been taken off now since we started back in 2017.

We had a huge pipeline, there's now hundreds of machines, thousands worldwide, up to about a hundred or more companies in America, and we were the third. The relationships were strong to continue to grow and we built everything from single family homes, to four-story, six-story pharmaceutical facilities, all non-combustible, complicated roof lines, houses on islands where we barged stuff over and helicoptered certain materials up over a hill that did not have any access, all kinds of amazing projects and great clients. However, the goal was always to build community.

What I didn't yet know, was the importance in food integration. What Plarr always did talk about was a safe way to live and have control of your community, including mechanical backups if there was ever a power breakdown, that you could survive and live and be safe. Seeing that there are farm-to-table communities around the world, it's not something new. It's actually something very old and it makes sense. Even from a marketability standpoint, it makes tons of sense. People want this, they want to live this way.

The Modi government in India needed a Canadian partner because of all the corruption going on. They had hunted us for going over to do a project back in 2019, and having the name Krishna didn't hurt as a partner. I personally went over there with him and we built a factory in 21 days. We trained a bunch of guys that couldn't even speak English, some young guys with a ton of heart, on how to run the machines and build their own homes, and run the factory that now can produce 4 million square ft. a year. We were supposed to go back and build many more factories, we also had a good friend who lost his home in the Malibu fires, Darin Olien of Superlife, who has a great show on Netflix called *Down to Earth*, and that was featured on the show. I personally walked the land with him after he lost his home and saw his electric motorcycle reduced to an artistic pile of aluminum. The one wooden house and all the trees burned, but the trees survived and the house died. The house was gone, like many, but the trees have moisture, so they actually tend to be okay. Hence, another huge value of what we do is the: *no bugs, no mold, no fire*. This has resonated with a lot of people. The non-combustible insurance savings is huge too.

People get the steel but they always ask us for more. Through Darin, we met Jim Gale, and we found our answer. He was recommended to meet us which was a great relationship. Before that, when the world shut down, after speaking at a conference in Los Angeles on January 26, 2020, we actually decided we were going to either go back to India or move on into the states. We did a deal to exit our company LifeTec Construction Group in Vancouver Canada, and it's still running today to the partners that took over and bought it. I was speaking at the conference when Kobe's helicopter went down. I was in the air space landing in Los Angeles, and the next day all the news said Kobe died. I was on a panel at a green conference and the newspaper that came out, had a tiny little thing that said COVID-19 which no one had heard about yet. As we were deciding what to do between the opportunity in California with all the fires and bringing a great product, or going back to India, things quickly changed as the world quickly shut down. Krishna went with a modular partner, one of our other partners built a six-story building on site with a machine on site, and Krishna went with an old friend and helped convert their modular company into steel. I personally went and helped build some beautiful luxury homes on an island called Keats Island, near where they shot a famous Canadian TV show back. I spent that summer watching the whales and building another beautiful couple of homes there for a great client. Then the phone started to ring as the machines are made in New Zealand, they were shut down more than most. For the machines that were sent to America, it was during the height of COVID, so they had no one to work through the start-up phase with all the companies and individuals that bought them. I got a phone call asking if I could help.

Being born in Alaska and being quite affected by what I felt was a little bit of overboard, dare I say, approaching tyranny, with the push *forcing* everyone toward certain medical choices, I did not personally agree with this. I saw it through a lot of Canada, being pretty heavy on the media push, and something was going on there. I was happy to see if I could get into the states with my American citizenship, being born there as a dual citizen, it had never been a problem before. They welcomed me in, I was the only one at the border in my vehicle. I made the track and crossed over, met up with an old friend in Denver who has the same mission as me and bought 200 Acres with an underground missile compound, also looking at restructuring the industrial military complex. As Buckminster Fuller says, don't try to change the old, make the new so that the old becomes obsolete. Then I met a great couple of brothers in Boston who had just received their framecad machines, and with all of the COVID restrictions, they were surprised to see me although I had been told by the company that makes the machines that they could use my help. I walked in the door and was welcomed, as I turned the machines on and started teaching them how they work and was confident in their ability as they were a lot like us when we started our company in Vancouver. We spent a few months there and was offered a partnership but Boston was very cold. Another company down in Florida in the

Panhandle had received machines and many others, but after making my way to Florida and reconnecting with Adam Good, through Darren Olien, we had gotten contacted by Jim Gale.

When Adam told me there was this off-grid community that wanted to talk to us about building it, I said "isn't that our dream?" Thinking back to being on a frozen oil rig up in Canada talking to my old friend about how one day we wanted to do this and really believed in it, it really struck me. I immediately drove out there as Adam did with Robert Plarr and I met Jim. I never looked back. It was a dream project from the beginning. Learning about the importance of food and seeing things like the storms in Texas shutting down whole communities, people literally dying because of it, it's become such an even more important mission of community and family. All of the layers of importance for this mission that we had to have multiple communities that we can travel between, as a type of club or whatever it ends up being, the mission stays the same though the names can change. The core is there, we have a system that works for building and teaching. My own daughter has done the work, my father in his 70s has also been able to learn and put this system together. We partnered with a great company that has nationwide manpower called CMR, so as a company we can deploy nationwide with our facility partnerships for the steel, as well as our install teams across the country. Now with what I've learned is way more important, the food growth actually is very important with the poisons we face. Jim's mission to turn lawns into food resonates together with our work as we have the total package.

Anything from a single home to a whole city, we can design digitally and print with any of our partnerships and install nationwide. We believe we've got a great partnership and tool that we can give to anyone who wants to use it, learn and build teams across America to build these communities. It is so important to have all facets with the Council of 12 integration of soil, with the livestock with Joel Salatin, with the mental health needs and a hero growing up in Calgary and the oil rigs being hockey player Theo Fleury, we have so many great personalities and individuals on this team and the mission will continue. We were able to build out the first phase of Galt's Landing. The correlation with Atlas Shrugged, the character named Galt, I have a grandson who my daughter named Atlas, we have a mission, a duty and a responsibility to work positively. A great friend from the film industry coined a term that I like to use, his name is Michael, he tells us it's not "I have a nightmare, it's I have a dream." You have to lead with positivity and not guilt or shame, although we may be in a tough time. There is a light and we can keep shining it. I'm so grateful to be a part of this team and do what I can to add to it. Even if you didn't believe in this, the marketability, the insurance savings, the fact that everyone wants to live like this, will not change. It's our mission to grow this across the world, thank you.

By McKinley Hlady

www.newenergyworld.net

These individuals came together and gathered their resources to create the Shared Earth, detailing the strategy that will change the world, and save it from it's current evils.

They are demonstrating the path that will inspire us, to secure the world based on life, rather than evil, for generations to come.

We begin with thoughts, then our emotions and our actions. From Natural Intelligence, showing by example, we arrive at the voluntary world based on permaculture ethics.

"Know well what leads you forward and what holds you back, and choose the path that leads to wisdom. **There are only two mistakes one can make along the road to truth; not going all the way, and not starting.** No one saves us but ourselves. No one can and no one may. We ourselves must walk the path." – Buddha

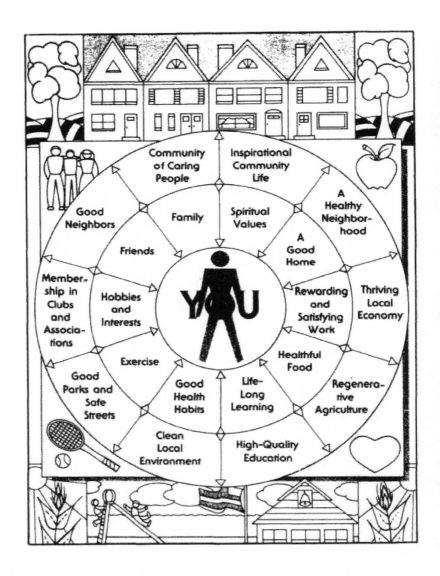

Photo From "The Voluntaryist" Magazine
(voluntaryist.com)

The Start:

"There is one thing stronger than all the armies in the world, and that is an idea whose time has come" - Victor Hugo. **What is the idea?**

"Whatever the mind can conceive and believe, it can achieve."- Napoleon Hill. **Was he wrong?**

"Though the problems of the world are increasingly complex, the solutions remain embarrassingly simple."- Bill Mollison. **What are the embarrassingly simple solutions?**

"You never change things by fighting the existing reality. To change something, build a new model that makes the existing model obsolete"- Buckminster Fuller. **What is the new model?**

"Everybody does the best they can with what they got, based on all things considered"- NLP. **What is the best we can do?**

"Those who love peace must learn to organize as effectively as those who love war"- Martin Luther King, Jr. **How do we organize to share an idea?**

"None are more hopelessly enslaved than those who falsely believe they are free."- Johnny Wolfgang von Goethe. **How could we know that we are free?**

"Know thyself, know thy enemy. A thousand battles, a thousand victories."- Sun Tzu. **Who am I?**

"The Spirit of the perennial spring is said to be immortal, she is called the Mysterious One."- Lao Tzu. **What do we truly serve?**

The Path:

1. Create awareness (inc. Permaculture & Voluntaryism)

2. Influencers organize (inc. Exampling, Shout-outs)

3. Call out and invite the corporations which are selling poisons to sell LIFE INSTEAD OF DEATH

Start planting seeds in all ways, always.

Engage in thoughts, engage in nature.

Share the ideas, share the fruits.

Share this book, rate this online.

Let everyone know, to know thyself.

Learn about those who are implementing and supporting projects, organizations and more, based on the solution Collaborate with us!

FoodForestAbundance.com

Learn about the movement representing the education of nature in all aspects of life

nita.one

A great way to support us and this mission:

GiveSendGo.com/NaturalIntelligence

GaltsLanding.Farm

TheLiberator.us

The Fruits:

Approximate Locations

Made in the USA
Columbia, SC
12 December 2024

8ba1c928-f04d-464d-8acd-cca6323ab9ccR02